The Punishment of the Stingy and Other Indian Stories

by
George Bird Grinnell

Introduction by Jarold Ramsey

University of Nebraska Press
Lincoln and London

Introduction copyright © 1982
by the University of Nebraska Press
All rights reserved
Manufactured in the United States of America

First Bison Book printing: May 1982
Most recent printing indicated by the first below:
3   4   5   6   7   8   9   10

Reprinted from the original
1901 edition published by Harper & Brothers

Library of Congress Cataloging in Publication Data
Grinnell, George Bird, 1849–1938.
The punishment of the stingy,
and other Indian stories.
Reprint. Originally published:
New York: Harper, 1901.
Includes bibliographical references.
1. Indians of North America—Fiction. I. Title.
PS1764.G774P8   1982   813'.52   81–21922
ISBN 0–8032–2113–4   AACR2
ISBN 0–8032–7008–9 (pbk.)

∞

INTRODUCTION
by Jarold Ramsey

George Bird Grinnell is one of the indispensable men of
the American West, a man of so many timely parts and
good offices that it would be beyond us to invent him, as
the saying goes, if we had to. How one man, born in
Brooklyn in that auspicious year 1849, turns out to be a
paleontologist, a noted explorer, a naturalist, a distinguished ethnologist, a best-selling author, a business
executive, one of the founders of both the Audubon Society and the Bronx Zoo, a planner and protector of Yel-
lowstone and Glacier national parks, long-time editor of
Forest and Stream, a famous big-game hunter and friend
of U.S. presidents, and a pioneer conservationist who
among other accomplishments brought about the federal
regulation of America's migratory game birds—how one
life manages to cover so much so well is a great mystery,
and it is tempting to think of this career and a few others
like it as representing a peculiar nineteenth-century
American mystery of opportunity and energy.

Indeed, it takes nothing away from Grinnell's mag-
nitude to observe how closely his achievements were
factored to the special openings and closings of his own
age. As John F. Reiger has written, none of the man's
considerable native talents and advantages were to be as
important to him "as the fact that in a little more than a
decade, he had witnessed the passing of the Great West."[1]
In the mythologies of the Plains Indians that Grinnell

knew intimately, there is a narrative formula known as "the lightning door." A hero, en route to his adventures, manages to get ahead of lightning and rides or leaps through its magic portal unscathed. So Grinnell: it was his fortune (and one imagines his burden) to experience at first hand in action the aboriginal West, and the course of the mountain men through it. But the wonderful door that opened for him in 1870, as a member of Yale Professor Othniel Marsh's great Darwinian geological expedition west of the Platte, had closed forever, he saw, by 1883— railroads and telegraph lines stitching the prairies, the buffaloes gone, fields plowed and fenced, reservations and agencies, Omaha, Lincoln, Denver . . . . How had it all passed? As suddenly and terribly as lightning.

One of Grinnell's great virtues as a conservationist (in the best and broadest sense) is that he kept his tragic vision of the Old West steady and whole, without sentimentalizing or exploiting it. Thus, in his forty years of ethnographic study and writing among the Pawnees, Blackfeet, Cheyennes, and their neighbors ("field work" hardly describes it), he never utters a "Lo the poor vanishing redskins"—although he keenly and often eloquently records what is being lost from the old ways of the tribes. Here is Grinnell explaining to Chief White Eagle why he is visiting the Pawnees in 1888 (a visit that no doubt yielded some of the stories in this book): "Father, we have come down here to visit the people and to talk to them; to ask them about how things used to be in the olden times, to hear their stories, to get their history, and then to put all these things down in a book, so that in the years to come, after the tribes have all become like white people, the old things of the Pawnees shall not be forgotten."[2]

Happily, today's Pawnees have not "all become like white people" by any means, but in the years since Grin-

INTRODUCTION

nell wrote *Pawnee Hero Stories and Folk Tales* and his other books, the value of his kind of practical historical conservancy has been amply confirmed. They continue to be the most widely read books of their kind; they have served us well, Anglos and Indians, scholars and general readers.

This is not to say that Grinnell's writings are without limitations. A movement is now underway in literary and anthropological circles to reexamine the mythologies of the North American Indians and bring about their recognition as literary art. Looked at from the rigorous perspectives of this "ethnopoetic" movement, in which ethnology, philology, linguistics, and semiotics all play a part, it must be conceded that Grinnell's "Indians stories" leave something to be desired on the score of textual authenticity. They were told and transcribed, first of all, in English, already one remove from the classical circumstances of their tribal existence. Although he knew the Cheyenne, Blackfeet, and Pawnee languages, Grinnell was not a linguist, and he offers no native-language texts; it is impossible to know what has been lost from, or added to, the narratives as the Indians knew them. To someone who is familiar with the Plains repertories from other sources, Grinnell's texts are notably lacking in bawdy and scatological elements—did his Indian raconteurs censor themselves on his behalf?

In each of his prefaces, Grinnell insists upon the scrupulous rendering of the stories *as told;* and as long as we acknowledge what is surely lost in them of native style and texture, there is no reason to doubt him. They are faithful, for example, to the native fondness for magical narrative repetition; Grinnell knew, as most editors of his time did not, that for an event to happen four or five times in succession was to native audiences not an exercise in tedious emphasis, but rather an important structuring of the story. Likewise, his stories are faithful to the native oral-narrative conventions that apparently precluded flashbacks, interruptions, shifts in point of view, authorial intrusion, or other narrative disruptions.

One does wish, given Grinnell's uniquely friendly relations with his favorite tribes, that he had revealed more about the circumstances of the story-recitals he heard, and about the dramatic methods of the recitalists. But against these obscurities it is only fair to set the appealing directness and vividness of the stories themselves—if not recreations of what the Indians heard and cherished, they do read like what skilled narrators might make of their complex traditions for a trusted Anglo friend, in English. And, as generations of scholars and general readers can testify, they are wonderfully rich in cultural details, superbly rendered *in action*—the well-bred shyness of the Piegan girl who encourages her poor suitor but also says, "And now go; people are looking at us" (p. 204 in this book); the origins of the ritual connection of corn and buffalo among the Pawnees (pp. 69–70); the ministrations of a Blood medicine man in "The Blindness of Pi-wáp-ōk" (pp. 144–47).

The distinguished anthropologist Ruth Bunzel has written in praise of Grinnell's books on the Cheyennes that in reading them "one can smell the buffalo grass and the wood fires, feel the heavy morning dew on the prairie"[3]—and in all his writings he manifests an all-too-rare ability to transmit his knowledge of a culture in terms of living details, not systematized facts. Something of the richness of Grinnell's ethnological knowledge is illustrated in a fascinating article he wrote for the *Journal of American Folklore* in 1892, in which he demonstrated that a well-known Pawnee myth about a magical person who could "call buffalo" to the hunters was in fact a mythifica-

tion of a common hunting practice among the faraway
northern Blackfeet, whereby hunters actually played on
the buffaloes' curiosity to lure them into chutes and cor-
rals for the killing.[4] Knowing both tribes well, he saw that
what was practical technology for one had been
reimagined as myth by the other—does such a process
account for other "magical" features in Indian
mythologies?

Grinnell himself never uses the terms "literature" and
"art" to magnify his mythic texts, nor does he venture to
comment on their possible complexities, or their merits,
as literary art. They are simply "tales" and "stories" to
him; their value being, in his view, chiefly ethnological
and historical. As he wrote, characteristically, in 1911:
"When we think that the tales these old men can relate
constitute the only history of the tribes we can ever obtain,
it is greatly to be regretted that more of them cannot be
collected and preserved."[5] There is nothing to be regretted, certainly, about his contributions to the preserving of
that history: and when his texts do offer something more
than cultural documentation—his version of the Blackfoot
"Old Man" cycle, for example, is one of the great creation
narratives in its very simplicity—we are reminded that the
native American myth repertories were oral *literatures,*
sources of spiritual and imaginative power to those who
knew them, as well as lore and entertainment.

The Punishment of the Stingy and Other Indian Stories
(1901) is an intriguing book because in editing it, Grinnell
does seem to have stepped closer to a recognition of the
literary merits of his material. First, there is the curious
book-trade aegis under which the work appeared: it was
the fifth volume in Harper's "Portrait Collection of Short
Stories," of which the first was William Dean Howells's *A
Pair of Patient Lovers.* Then, too, it is his only collection to

embrace narratives from a number of tribes (Blackfoot, Pawnee, Blood, Piegan, and the Northwest Chinooks, far out of his usual territory), a detail that suggests in itself other than ethnographic purposes; and he seems to have selected and arranged the texts in anthology fashion according to the related themes of stinginess and generosity, and the emergence out of obscurity of plucky, generous young heroes—native analogues, as it were, to the Horatio Alger formula.

The style, however, is consistent for the most part with the two tribal collections he had already published, on the Pawnees and the Blackfeet—that is, simple, direct, untextured. If we are nowadays inclined to regret, in the name of ethnopoetics, the exclusion of authentic details of style-in-performance, we have cause to be grateful that Grinnell, unlike most of the popular anthologists of the time, refused to embellish his materials or to impose a false Anglo literary manner on them. A glance at the mannered Victorian style of the contents of Daniel Brinton's various native collections, or the stories of the Sioux author Charles Eastman in *Red Hunters and the Animal People* (1905), will underscore the plain virtues of Grinnell's method in this and his other collections.

If Grinnell's work has its own integrity, it also bears an authentic relationship to the corpus of native American traditional literatures as we know them from other sources. That relationship can be seen in the following notes:

"The Blue Jay Stories"—Clatsop Chinook

These stories were evidently collected near the mouth of the Columbia River during a trip by Grinnell to the Northwest in the 1890s. Grinnell's laudatory note (p. x) on the work of Franz Boas suggests that these texts may owe something to Boas's *Chinook Texts*, Twentieth Annual

INTRODUCTION

Report of the Bureau of American Ethnology, XX (1894).
At any rate, Boas gives a native-language text and a trans-
lation of each of these stories, as follows: "The Punishment of the Stingy," *Chinook Texts*, cf. Boas pp. 132 ff.;
"Bluejay the Imitator," ibid., pp. 172 ff.; "Bluejay Visits
the Ghosts," ibid., pp. 153 ff.

Comparison of the two sets of texts reveals Boas's to be
much more difficult to read according to Anglo narrative
conventions, but likewise much more expressive of a dis-
tinctive native literary style. (Boas's informant, Charles
Cultee, was in fact a gifted storyteller, a literary artist in
his own right.) One of these "trickster" stories, "Bluejay
the Imitator" in Grinnell's version, follows a widely dis-
tributed Indian comic narrative motif, "The Bungling
Host"; see examples and citations in Stith Thompson, ed.,
Tales of the North American Indians (Bloomington: In-
diana University Press, 1968).

"The Girl Who Was the Ring," "The Star Boy," "The First Corn," and "The Grizzly Bear's Medicine"—Pawnee

For versions of "The Girl Who Was the Ring" and "The
Star Boy," based on transcriptions from the Pawnee lan-
guage, see George A. Dorsey, *Traditions of the Skidi
Pawnee, Memoirs of the American Folklore Society*, vol. 8
(1904), pp. 254 ff. and 60 ff., respectively. The "Star Boy"
motif is widespread on the Plains; see N. Scott Momaday's
Kiowa telling of it in *The Way to Rainy Mountain* (New
York: Ballantine Books, 1970).

"The First Medicine Lodge"—Piegan

See Grinnell's very detailed Blackfoot version, "Scarface," in *Blackfoot Lodge Tales*, pp. 93–104. In this version, the rags-to-riches hero becomes a star in the sky,
rather than just a permanent guest in Sun's house. For

INTRODUCTION

another Piegan telling of this popular story, see Clark Wissler and D. C. Duvall, *"Mythology of the Blackfoot Indians, Anthropological Papers of the American Museum of Natural History,* vol. 2, (1908), pp. 61–65. Apropos of such intertribal variations, characteristic of oral literatures in general and of Plains Indian traditions in particular, Wissler and Duvall quote a Blood storyteller: "The venerable old man pulled up a common ragweed, saying, 'The parts of this weed all branch off from the stem. They go different ways, but all come from the same root. So it is with the different versions of a myth' " (p. 5).

> "Thunder Maker and Cold Maker," "The Blindness of Pi-wáp-ok," "Ragged Head," "Nothing Child," "Shield Quiver's Wife," "The Beaver Stick," "Little Friend Coyote"—Blackfoot

These stories come from Grinnell's extensive association with the Blackfeet (after 1895 he was U.S. commissioner for their affairs), but the second and third stories feature Blood, and Nez Perce and Piegan, protagonists, respectively, reminding us again of the extensive dissemination of stories, motifs, and characters between tribes. A short variant of "The Beaver Stick" is given by Wissler and Duvall, in fact, as a North Piegan text (*Mythology of the Blackfoot Indians,* pp. 76–77). Apart from the Scarface story and an analogue of "The Beaver Stick" ("The Beaver Medicine," pp. 117–24), there is little overlap between these narratives and those in Grinnell's *Blackfoot Lodge Tales.*

"Ragged Head" and "Shield Quiver's Wife" are naturalistic in their details and appear to be historical narratives, dating from the mid-nineteenth century, when the

INTRODUCTION

Plains and Rocky Mountain nations (and the Nez Perces and Cayuses of the Far West) were devoted to conducting daring raids on each other for horses and glory. For a typical narrative of this sort (Cayuse), see "How Fish-Hawk Raided the Sioux" in Jarold Ramsey, ed., *Coyote Was Going There: Indian Literature of the Oregon Country* (Seattle: University of Washington Press, 1977), pp. 25–27.

For readers interested in placing these stories comparatively within the general field of native American mythology, the best comprehensive gathering of myth-narratives is still Stith Thompson's *Tales of the North American Indians.* Thompson's bibliography is especially valuable as a survey of scholarly work done among the Great Plains Indians by Grinnell's contemporaries. The aims and methods of the work now underway on Indian texts *as* literature are illustrated in Karl Kroeber, ed., *Traditional Literatures of the American Indian: Texts and Interpretations* (Lincoln: University of Nebraska Press, 1981). Dell Hymes's "Discovering Oral Performance and Measured Verse in American Indian Narratives," *New Literary History* 8 (Spring 1977): 431–57, is already a classic in this new field of literary interpretation.

The history of the Plains Indians as we have it would be unthinkable without the keen eye and honest, diligent pen of George Bird Grinnell. With him, it is still possible after eighty or one hundred years to leap through that historical lightning-door that shut so suddenly on the Old West. Amongst the heroic Pawnees, Cheyennes, Blackfeet, and their neighbors of long ago, stories like these will continue to be our horses, and Grinnell our faithful overland guide.

INTRODUCTION

NOTES

1. John F. Reiger, ed., *The Passing of the Great West: Selected Papers of George Bird Grinnell* (New York: Winchester Press, 1972), p. 152. For Grinnell's role as a pioneer conservationist, see Reiger's *American Sportsmen and the Origins of Conservation* (New York: Winchester Press, 1975). Professor Reiger is now (1981) writing a biography of Grinnell.

2. *Pawnee Hero Stories and Folk-Tales* (1889; reprint ed. Lincoln: University of Nebraska Press, 1961), pp. 5–6.

3. Ruth Bunzel, in Bunzel and Margaret Mead, *The Golden Age of American Anthropology* (New York: G. Braziller, 1960), p. 114.

4. "Development of a Pawnee Myth," *Journal of American Folklore* 5 (1892): 127 ff.

5. *The Indians of Today* (New York: Duffield and Co., 1911), p. 39.

Contents

Illustrations

The Stories and the Story-Tellers

HE stories in this book deal with peoples of widely different surroundings and habit — some with dwellers on the sea - shore, whose skies are often obscured by rain and fog, who draw their living from the sea, and are at home on the water; and others with inhabitants of the high plains, where the air is pure and dry, and the summer sun is rarely hidden by clouds.

As the Indians have no written characters, memorable events are retained only in the minds of the people, and are handed down by the elders to their children, and by these again transmitted to their children, so passing from generation to generation. Until recent years, one of the sacred duties of certain elders of the tribes was the handing down of these histories to their successors. As they repeated them, they impressed upon the hearer the importance of remembering the stories precisely as told, and of telling them again exactly as he had received them, neither adding nor taking away anything. Thus early taught his duty, each listener strove to perform it, and to impress on those whom he in turn instructed a similar obligation.

In transcribing stories such as these, care must be used to take down just what the narrator says. The stories must be reproduced as they are told; otherwise they lose that primitive flavor which is often one of their chief charms. In their true form they are full of human nature, full of unconscious suggestion as to how the primitive mind worked, and full also of hints as to the customs and life of the people in the old days.

Seated by the flickering fire in Blackfoot skin-lodge, or in Pawnee dirt-house, or in sea-shore dwelling on the northwest coast, I have received these stories from the lips of aged historians, and have set them down here as I have heard them.

The Bluejay Stories

O N the shores of the ocean which washes our northwest coast live many tribes of a hardy, seafaring people. Their houses stand along the beach just above high-water mark, and behind them the wooded mountains rise sharply. The waters at their feet yield them the chief share of their living. The salmon that each year come to the rivers to spawn, the great shoals of little herrings that visit the beach, the halibut that lie at the bottom far at sea, the seals, the sea-lions, the porpoises, and the whales, all provide something towards the tribe's support. Or, if for a while all these fail, there are flat-fish on the shoals, clams in the mud flats, and mussels clinging to the rocks. In the stories told by this race of seafarers, the incidents have to do with the common events of their lives, and the scenes are commonly laid on the water or at the water's edge. Thus they treat of the hunting of the sea-lion, of the catching of the salmon, most often of the search for food

Most of the stories to be related here are very old, and date from a period when men and animals were far more closely related than they seem to be to-day; when, as the tales clearly show, each could understand the other's language, and when friendly intercourse between them was common. Although in recent years all the conditions of the lives of these people have changed, stories such as these may still be heard, if one can gain the confidence of the aged men and women who yet retain this legendary lore. In somewhat different form, the Bluejay Stories, in the original tongue, may be found in the Chinook Texts, collected by that eminent ethnologist, Dr. Franz Boas, whose studies of American tribes have yielded such important and valuable results.

The Punishment of the Stingy

A BLUEJAY STORY

The Punishment of the Stingy

A T Sea Side lived many people—a big village. Their houses were on the bank, and, below, the wide beach sloped down to the salt water. Under the bank the canoes rested on the beach above high-water mark. Beyond was the sea.

One day the Chief of the village died. He had one son, a big boy just growing up to be a man. It was winter, and the people had hardly anything to eat. They looked along the beach for food cast up by the sea, but they could find nothing. They were hungry, and did not know what they should do. Mussels and roots were their only food.

One day a hunter said to the men: "Everybody get ready; let us go out to sea. Perhaps there we may find something to eat; even if we kill nothing, we can at least gather mussels."

3

The Punishment of the Stingy

So all the men got ready, and they started out to sea in two canoes. After they had gone some distance they came to a small island, and saw there some sea-lions, and the hunter speared one, and it jumped out to the water and swam strongly, and then it died and floated on the water. They dragged it up on the shore near by, and Bluejay said, "We will boil it here." So they made a fire there and singed it and cut it up and boiled it. Then Bluejay said: "Let us eat it here. Let us eat all of it, and not take any of it home with us." So these people ate there. The Raven wished to take home some of the meat to give to persons who were hungry, and hid a piece in his mat and carried it to the canoe, but Bluejay ran down and took the meat and threw it into the fire and burned it. After they had eaten all they wanted, they made ready to go home. They gathered mussels, large and small. In the evening they came to the village, and Bluejay called out to his wife, "Stikuá, come and get your mussels." There was a noise of many feet as Stikuá and the other women came running down to get their mussels, and carried them up to the houses.

4

The Punishment of the Stingy

The Raven took care of the Chief's son. That night the boy said to him, " To-morrow I want to go with you." Bluejay said: " What are you going to do? The waves will carry you away. You will be washed away. I was almost washed away."

Early the next morning the men made ready to go hunting again. They went down to the beach and got into the canoes, and the boy also went down to the beach. He intended to go with them, and as they were pushing off he tried to get into one of the canoes. Bluejay said to him: " Go up to the houses. Go up to the houses." The boy went, as he had been told, but he felt very sorry, and then Bluejay said, " Quick, let us leave him." The people began to paddle.

At length they reached the land where they had been the day before. It was a rocky island. The hunter went ashore and speared a sea-lion. They hauled it to the shore and pulled it up on land, and then pulled it up away from the beach. Bluejay said, " We will eat it all here, or else our Chief's son will always be wanting to come with us." So now they singed the sea-lion, and cut it up and boiled it

The Punishment of the Stingy

there. Then, when what they were cooking
was ready, they ate plenty. The Raven tried
to save one piece of the meat. He tied it in
his hair, intending to hide it, but Bluejay took
it out and threw it into the fire and burned it.
When they started home they gathered mussels,
and at evening they got home. Before they
landed, Bluejay called out loud, "Come,
Stikuá, and get your mussels." There was a
noise of feet running, and Stikuá and her children came running to the beach with all the
other women. Then they carried the mussels
up to the houses. Bluejay said to the men who
had been with him, "Do not tell the Chief's
son, any of you, for if you do he will always
go with us."

That night the boy said, "To-morrow I am
going with you"; and Bluejay said to him:
"What are you going to do? You may drift
away. You may be overwhelmed by the
waves." The boy said, "I will go with you."

On the third morning they rose early and
went to the beach, and the boy also went to the
beach, and took hold of the side of the canoe
to get in. Bluejay said: "What are you doing
here? Go to the houses." The boy cried, but

6

he went back. Then Bluejay said to the others, " Quick, paddle; we will leave him behind." Then the people paddled away. At length they arrived at the rock of the sea -lions, and the hunter went ashore. He speared a large sea - lion, and pretty soon it floated dead on the water. They pulled it in to the shore and up on the beach, and then they hauled it up above the beach and singed and cut it up and boiled it there. When it was done they ate, and Bluejay said: " We will eat it all. We will not tell any one, for fear that our Chief's son should want to come with us." After all had eaten enough, a little meat was still left. The Raven tried to hide a piece of it. He tied it to his leg and put a bandage over it, and said that his leg was broken. Bluejay burned all the meat that was left over. He said to the Raven, " I want to see your leg." He seized the Raven's leg and untied it, and found the piece of meat that the Raven had tied to it and burned it. Towards evening they gathered mussels, and then they went home.

When they were nearly at their home Bluejay called out, " Stikuá, your mussels." There was a noise of feet, and Stikuá and the women ran to the beach. They carried the mussels up from the beach and ate mussels all night. The boy said, " To-morrow, I think, I shall surely go along with you." Bluejay said to him: " What are you going to do? You will drift away. I should have drifted away twice if I had not caught hold of the canoe."

Early the next morning they made themselves ready, and the boy got up and made himself ready. Then the people hauled their canoes down to the water and got into them. The boy tried to get into a canoe too, but Bluejay took hold of him and threw him into the water. He stood in the water up to his waist. He took hold of the side of the canoe, but Bluejay hit his hands to make him let go. For a long time he held on, and cried and cried, but at last he let go and went up to the house. Then Bluejay and the other people paddled away. After a while they reached the rock where the sea-lions lived, and the hunter went ashore and speared a sea-lion, and it jumped into the water and soon floated there dead. Then they towed it to the beach and pulled it up and singed it, and cut it up and boiled it. Bluejay

"HE SAW A BALD-HEADED EAGLE"

The Punishment of the Stingy

said, "We will eat it here." They ate for a long time and ate half of it, and then they were satisfied. They were so full that they went to sleep. After a while Bluejay awoke and burned all the meat that was left. Towards evening they gathered mussels and then started home.

When they were near the shore, Bluejay called out to his wife, " Come and get your mussels, Stikuá," and they heard the noise of feet running down to the shore. Then they carried up the mussels from the beach. That night the boy said, " To-morrow I shall go with you "; and Bluejay said to him: " What are you going to do? We may be thrown into the water and you may drown."

Early the next morning the men made ready to start. The boy also got up and made himself ready. Then Bluejay and the people hauled the canoes down to the water and got into them. The boy tried to get into the canoe, but Bluejay threw him into the water, and they pushed off. The boy caught hold of the side of the canoe and held it. He stood there in the water up to his armpits, and tried to get into the canoe, but Bluejay hit his hands and made him

9

let go. The boy cried and cried. Bluejay and the people paddled away.

After a little time the boy went up to the beach, feeling very sad, and trying to think what he should do. At last he went into the house and took his arrows and started, walking along the shore. He walked around a point, and saw a black eagle, and shot it. He skinned it and tried to put the skin on his body, but it was too small. It did not reach down as far as his knees. He took it off and left it there and went on. After a while he saw another eagle, and he shot it, and it fell down. Its head was partly white. He skinned it and put the skin on his body, but it was too small. It reached down only a little below his knees. Then he took it off and left it lying there, and went on a long way. At last he saw a bald-headed eagle. He shot it, and it fell down. Then he skinned it and put the skin on himself. Even this was too small, but it nearly fitted him. Then he tried to fly. At first he could only fly downward. He could not rise in the air. He tried again, and this time he found that he could turn, so he kept on trying, and pretty soon he could fly well.

"THE BIRD CAME DOWN"

The Punishment of the Stingy

Now he flew towards the village, and when he had come near to this point he smelled smoke, and in that smoke he smelled fat cooking. So before he got to the village he turned and flew out to sea, following the smell of the smoke. Pretty soon he came to the rock of the sealions, and there he saw the men of his village. He lit on a tree far off and watched them, looking down on them below. He saw that they were cooking, and when the meat was done he saw them eating. When they had nearly finished eating, he flew towards them, and he thought, " I wish Bluejay would see me." Bluejay did see the bird flying, and he said, " Ha! a bird is coming to get food from us." The boy flew around them once, and then again. Five times he circled around them, all the time coming lower. Bluejay took a piece of meat and threw it out, and said to the bird, " I give you this to eat; take it." The bird came down, and, grasping the piece of meat, flew away. Then Bluejay said, " Why, that bird has feet just like a person!"

When Bluejay and the people had finished eating they went to sleep. Again the Raven hid a piece of meat. Towards evening Bluejay

11

awoke, and then the people ate again, and afterwards Bluejay burned what they had left. Then they gathered mussels and started to go home. When they were close to the houses Bluejay called out, " Ah, Stikuá, get your mussels." All the women ran down to the beach with a noise of feet, and carried up the mussels.

When the boy got home he at once lay down. That evening the people tried to wake him, but he did not rise.

The next morning, as soon as it became day, early, they began to get ready, and again they hauled their canoes into the water. The Chief's son still lay in bed. He did not try to go with them, and they started off. After a while the sun rose. Then the boy got up. He called together all the women and children and said to them: " Quick, wash yourselves. Hurry; don't be lazy." They all washed themselves. Then he said, " Quick, comb your hair." They did so.

Then he put down a plank on the ground and took a piece of meat from under his blanket, and said to them, " All your husbands eat a great deal of this meat every day." He put two pieces of the meat side by side on the plank.

"FIVE TIMES HE CIRCLED AROUND THEM"

The Punishment of the Stingy

Then he cut off a piece of the meat and greased
the heads of all the women and the children.
Then he pulled out of the ground the wall
planks of the houses and sharpened them. If
a wall plank was wide, he split it. He sharpened all of them. The Raven's house was the
last house in the village. He did not pull down
its planks. He fastened the planks on the
backs of the women, and said to the women,
"Now go to the beach and swim towards the
sea, and as you go, swim five times around that
rock and then go out to sea. After this you
shall be killer whales. When you find sea-
lions you shall always kill them, but do not
give any of them to stingy people. When you
kill a good whale you shall eat it, but do not
give any of it to stingy people. I shall take
these children with me. They shall live on
the sea and be my relations." Then he began
to split sinews; he split a great many of them.
He threw down the sinews that he had split on
the stones where the people used to gather their
mussels, and said to the mussels, "After this
when Bluejay and these others go to take up
you mussels, you shall always be tied fast to
the rocks."

The Punishment of the Stingy

Now the women went down to the water's
edge and swam about, and began slowly to
jump out of the water. Five times they swam
backward and forward before the village; then
they went seaward, swimming very fast. They
kept on to the island where Bluejay and his
fellows were cooking their food. Bluejay said
to the men, " What is this that is coming?"
The men looked at the things that were coming,
and saw the women often jumping out of the
water. Five times they swam around that rock,
then they went out to sea. After a while birds
came flying after them towards the sea—birds
with red bills, just as if blood were on their
beaks. They kept following one another, many
of them. Bluejay said: " Do you see these
birds, how they keep coming? Where do they
come from?" Then the Raven said, " How is
it that you do not recognize these as your children?" Five times the birds flew around the
rock, just as the women had gone around it,
and then they flew away out to sea.

When Bluejay and his people were eating
the meat that they had killed, that hunter said:
" Quick, let us go home. I am afraid that we
have seen bad spirits. We never before saw

14

"THEN THEY WENT SEAWARD"

[See p. 14

anything like this at this rock." Then they
gathered some mussels, and put in the canoes
the meat that was left and carried it with them.
Just at evening they came to the village, and
Bluejay called out, " Ah, Stikuá, come and get
your mussels." There was no noise of people
running. Five times he called to her, but no
one came. It was all still. They went up on
the beach, and then they saw that no one was
there, and that the walls of the houses had disappeared. Then they began to cry, and Bluejay cried too. Some one said to him, " Be
quiet, Bluejay; if you had not been bad, our
Chief would not have done this to us."

Now they made only one house for all; all
lived together. Only the Raven, who had been
kind-hearted, had a house to himself. He often
went along the beach looking for food, and was
lucky, for sometimes he found a sturgeon; or
again he went along the beach looking for food
and he found a porpoise. Bluejay often went
along the beach trying to find food, but he was
always unlucky, for he found nothing, and
often, while he was looking, suddenly it would
begin to hail—big hailstones. Often he went
out to gather mussels and tried to break them

The Punishment of the Stingy

off from the rocks, but he could not do it. They were stuck fast to the stones. So he gave up and went home. He cried a great deal. Often the Raven looked for food along the beach and found a seal. The others had nothing to eat except roots.

Thus these men who had not brought food to their families had now lost their women and children, their houses had been pulled down and taken away, and they had nothing to eat. So their Chief punished them for being stingy.

Bluejay, the Imitator

Bluejay, the Imitator

BLUEJAY and his elder sister Ioí, with her five children, lived together in a house by the sea beach. Every morning they went out to walk along the beach, to see what the tide had washed up during the night that was good to eat. Sometimes they found fish, or a seal, and sometimes a whale. Some days when they found nothing, they dug clams on the flat, but some days they could get no clams, and so they were hungry. Up and down the shore lived their neighbors.

One day Bluejay said to his sister: " Let us go visiting; let us visit the Magpie." She said, " Let it be so. We will go."

Early next morning they put their canoe in the water and paddled away, and when they came near the Magpie's house they saw him sitting on the roof. They landed, and went up to the house, and the Magpie came down from the roof, and all went inside and sat down. Bluejay and his sister sat there and looked all around, but they saw no food. After a little while the Magpie swept his house, and while he was sweeping it out he found one dry salmon egg. He put this in the feathers of his head. Then he made a fire and heated some stones. He filled a basket - work kettle with water, put the salmon egg in the water, then put the stones in the water, one after another, and covered the kettle. Soon the water was boiling, and when it had boiled a little while he took off the cover, and the kettle was full of boiled salmon eggs. The Magpie put the kettle before Bluejay and his sister, and said, " Eat, my friends; you must be hungry." They ate until they were satisfied, and still the kettle was half full.

After a time they started to return to their house, taking with them the kettle with the food that was left. When they were about to start, his sister said to Bluejay, " You go down first to the beach." He said to her, " No, you go down first." So his sister went down first to the beach to get the canoe ready.

Bluejay, the Imitator

Bluejay said to the Magpie, "To - morrow come and visit us and get your kettle and bring it back with you." The Magpie said, "It is good; I will go to visit you." Then Bluejay and his sister went home.

The next morning, early, Bluejay went up on the roof of his house and sat there. After a time he called out to his sister, and said: "A canoe is coming." She answered: "It is coming, because you told him to come." Pretty soon, as they looked, they could see that it was the Magpie in the canoe, and at length he landed and pulled his canoe up on the beach and walked up to the house. Bluejay came down from the roof, and they went in and sat down.

Soon Bluejay got up and swept his house, and found one dry salmon egg, which he put in his topknot. When he had finished sweeping his house, he built a fire and heated some stones and filled a basket-work kettle with water and put in it the salmon egg, and then the hot stones, and covered the kettle. He did everything just as the Magpie had done it. Soon the water boiled, and he took the cover off, but there was nothing in the kettle but hot water.

The Magpie said, "Bluejay can do only one

thing." He took the kettle and threw the stones out of it. Then he heated more stones, put a dry salmon egg in the water, put in the hot stones, and covered the kettle, and soon the water began to boil. Presently he took the cover off the kettle, and it was full of boiled salmon eggs. Then the Magpie went down to the beach and put his canoe in the water and paddled away to his home.

After several nights Bluejay and his sister were hungry. Bluejay said: "Let us go visiting. Let us go and visit the Duck." "We will go to - morrow," said his sister. The next morning early they started and paddled away towards the Duck's house. After a while they came within sight of the house, and then landed on the beach and went up to the house. After they had sat a little while, the Duck said to her five children, "Go and wash yourselves." They went down to the beach and went into the water and washed themselves. Then they dived, and when each came to the top of the water it had a trout in its mouth. They put these on a mat on the beach. Ten times they dived, and by that time their mat was full of trout. They took

Bluejay, the Imitator

them up to the house and made a fire and
roasted them, and when the fish were cooked
they gave them to Bluejay and his sister, and
they ate part of them and were satisfied. Pretty
soon the visitors got ready to go, taking with
them the food that was left. Ioí said to her
brother: "You go down first to the beach, or
else you will talk ever so much." Bluejay answered her: "No, you go down first." So his
sister went down first to get the canoe ready,
and when she had gone, Bluejay said to the
Duck: "Come to my house to-morrow and get
your mat." The Duck said: "To-morrow I will
go to visit you." Then Bluejay and his sister
paddled away, and soon came to their house.

Early next morning Bluejay got up and went
up to the roof of the house. After he had been
sitting there for some time, he called out to his
sister: "A canoe is coming." She said to him:
"It comes because you asked them to come."
Pretty soon the Duck, with her five children,
reached the beach, and after they had pulled
the canoe out of the water, they went up to the
house. After they had sat a while, Bluejay
said to his sister's children: "Go and wash
yourselves."

The Punishment of the Stingy

The children went down to the beach and into the water and washed themselves. They tried to dive, but no matter how hard they might try their backs remained above the water. Ten times they tried to dive, and their feathers were all wet and clinging to them, and they were almost dead with cold. They came up to the house shivering, and not bringing anything with them.

The Duck said: " Bluejay can do only one thing." Then she said to her children: " Go and wash yourselves. We will give them something to eat." The Duck's children went down to the beach and washed themselves. They dived ten times, and then their mat was full of trout. They brought them up to the house and threw them on the ground. Then the Ducks went home.

Some little time after this Bluejay and his sister were again hungry. Bluejay said: " Let us go and visit Black Bear." Early the next morning they set out, and before noon they reached the Black Bear's house and went in and sat down.

They looked around. No food was to be seen. Pretty soon the Bear built a fire and be-

Bluejay, the Imitator

gan to heat stones. Bluejay was wondering
what food would be given them, and he said
to his sister: "What will he give us to eat?"

When the stones were hot the Bear took his
knife and cut the soles from his feet, and cut
a big piece of meat out of his thigh. Then he
rubbed his hands over the wounds, and at once
they were healed. Then he cut the flesh that
he had taken from his feet and from his thigh
into small pieces and put it in the kettle, and
put the hot stones in the kettle and boiled it.
When it was cooked he placed the kettle before
them, and said to them: "Eat, my friends; you
must be hungry." They ate, and pretty soon
they were satisfied. When they were ready to
go home Ioí said to her brother: "You go down
first, or else you will be talking a great deal."
Bluejay said: "No, you go down first." His
sister went, and when she had gone Bluejay
said to the Bear: "Come to-morrow and visit
us." The Bear said he would do so; then Bluejay and his sister went home to their house.

Early the next morning Bluejay got up and
made a fire, and went up on the roof of his
house. After a while, he called out to his sister: "A canoe is coming," and she answered:

The Punishment of the Stingy

"It comes because you invited him." Pretty soon the Bear paddled up to the beach and landed, and came up to the house, and they all sat down. Bluejay began to heat the stones in the fire and to get ready for cooking. When the stones were hot he sharpened his knife and began to cut his feet, but, oh, it hurt him very much. It hurt him so much that he fainted away. They blew on him until he recovered.

The Bear said: "You can do only one thing, Bluejay." The Bear took his knife and slowly cut the soles off his feet. He cut a piece of flesh out of his thigh. Then he rubbed his hands over the wounds and immediately they were healed. Then he cut the flesh in small pieces and boiled it. When he had finished cooking and it was done, he threw it down before them, and went home to his house. Bluejay's feet were sore.

After a number of nights they were again hungry. Then Bluejay said to his sister: "Let us go visiting again. To-morrow we will go and visit the Beaver." Early in the morning they started out, and before very long they reached the Beaver's house. The Beaver was on the roof of his house. He came down, and they went in and sat down. After a little while the Beaver went out and brought into the house a bundle of willow twigs, which he put down before them. Then he took a dish and went out and brought it back filled with mud. Bluejay and his sister could not eat these things, and pretty soon they got ready to go home. As they were about to start, his sister said to him: " You go down first to the beach, or else you will talk a great deal." The Bluejay said to his sister: " No, you go down first." So she went down first to the beach. When she had gone Bluejay said: " Come to my house to-morrow to fetch your dish," and the Beaver answered: " I will come to-morrow."

Early next morning Bluejay got up and made a fire, and went up on the roof of his house. After he had sat there for a while, he called out to his sister: " A canoe is coming." She answered: " It comes because you asked it to come." The Beaver landed and came up the beach and entered the house, and they all sat down. Bluejay went out of the house, and after he had been gone a little while he came back with a bunch of willow twigs, and he put them before the Beaver, who began to eat them, and soon ate them all up. Then Bluejay ran down to the beach and got some mud, which he put before the Beaver. The Beaver ate it all and went home.

Not many days after this they were again hungry, and Bluejay said: "Let us go visiting again. To-morrow let us go to visit the Seal." Early the next morning they started, and at length they came to the house of the Seal. The Seal had five children. After they had been sitting a while in her house, the Seal said to her children: "Go to the beach and lie down there." They went down to the edge of the water and lay there. Then the Seal took a stick and went down there, too, and when she reached her children she struck the youngest one on the head and it lay there. She said to the others: "Dive down," and they did so, and when they came to the surface of the water there were five of them. Then she dragged up to the house the one that she had killed and singed it, and when she had finished singeing it she cut it up. She boiled it, and when it was cooked she gave it to Bluejay and his sister. They ate, and presently they were satisfied. When they were getting ready to go home his

28

Bluejay, the Imitator

sister said to her brother: " You go down first."
He answered: " No, you go down first. You
always want to stay where they give us food."
So his sister went down to the beach. Then
Bluejay said to the Seal: " Come to-morrow and
visit us, and fetch your kettle." The Seal said:
" I shall come." Then Bluejay and his sister
went home to their house.

Early next morning Bluejay got up and went
on to the roof of his house. After a while he
called out to his sister: " A canoe is coming."
She answered him: " It comes because you have
asked them to come." The canoe came to the
beach, and the Seal and her children landed
and pulled the canoe up on the beach, and then
came up to the house. Pretty soon Bluejay
said to his sister's children: " Go to the beach
and lie down there." The children went and
lay down at the edge of the water. Bluejay
took a stick and went down and struck the
youngest one on the head. Then he said to
the other children: " Quick now, dive." They
dived, but when they came up there were only
four. Five times they dived, but the one that
Bluejay had struck remained dead. Then Ioí
and her children cried for the dead one.

The Punishment of the Stingy

The Seal said: "Bluejay only knows how to do one thing." She struck one of her daughters on the head with a stick, and said to the others: "Quick, dive." They dived, and when they came up again all five of them were there. Then she singed her daughter, and when she had finished singeing her she cut her up and threw her down before Bluejay and his sister, saying: "You may eat this." Then they tied up and buried the dead child, and the Seals went home.

After a time these two were again hungry, and Bluejay said: "Let us go and visit the Shadows." His sister said: "We will go to-morrow." Early next morning they started, and at last they reached the home of the Shadows and went up to the house. It was full of food, and on the beds there were lying ornaments, clothing, coats, blankets of deer skin, of mountain-goat wool, and of ground-hog skin. Bluejay said to his sister: "Where are these people?" His sister answered: "They are here, but you cannot see them."

Bluejay took up one of the large ear ornaments. "Look out! You are pulling my ear, Bluejay!" cried a person. Bluejay was surprised, for he saw no one, and he dropped the ear ornament. Then they heard many people laughing. He took hold of a ground - hog blanket, and pulled at it. "Let go of my ground - hog blanket, Bluejay," said a person, but he could see no one. He looked under the bed for the one who had spoken, and again they heard people laughing. He took up a coat made of goat wool, and somebody cried out, "Why do you lift my coat, Bluejay?" He took hold of a nose ornament, and a person cried, "Let go of my nose ornament, Bluejay." Then a basket fell down from above. He lifted it up and put it back. Then he began to look under the bed and all through the house for persons, and again they heard many people laughing. His sister said to him: "Stay here quietly. They are Shadows, and so you cannot see them." They ate some of the food.

When it got dark Bluejay said, "We will sleep here." So they slept there during the night, but all through the night they had bad dreams, for so the Shadows punished Bluejay, because he had teased them. Then Bluejay and his sister went home, and his sister said, "Now we have gone visiting enough."

Bluejay Visits the Ghosts

Bluejay Visits the Ghosts

I N a certain village there lived Ioí and her younger brother, Bluejay. One night the ghosts went out to buy a wife. They bought Ioí. The presents they gave for her were not sent back; they were kept. So at night she was married, and when day came Ioí was gone from her father's house. For a long time Bluejay did nothing; but at length he felt lonely, and after a year had passed he said, " I am going to look for my elder sister." He started for the country of the ghosts, and on his way he began to ask every one whom he saw, " Where does a person go when he dies?" He asked all the trees, but they could not tell him. He asked all the birds, but they could not tell him. At last he asked a Wedge, and the Wedge said, " If you will pay me, I will carry you there." He paid, and the Wedge carried him to the country of the ghosts.

They came to a large village, but no smoke rose from the houses; only from the last house —a big one—they saw smoke rising. Bluejay went into this house, and there he saw his elder sister. She said to him: "Ah, my younger brother, where do you come from? Are you dead?" He answered, "No, I am not dead; the Wedge brought me here on its back."

After a little Bluejay went out and walked through the village, and began to open the doors of the houses and to look into them; and when he looked into them he did not find people in any of the houses, but only bones. Then he came back to where his elder sister was. On the bed near where his sister was sitting lay a skull and some bones. He asked her, "What are you going to do with that skull and those bones?" She said to him, "That is my husband, your brother-in-law." Bluejay did not believe her; he said to himself: "Ioí is telling lies. She says a skull and bones is my brother-in-law!"

When it got dark people began to appear, and soon the house was full. It was a large

Bluejay Visits the Ghosts

house, but there were many people in it. Bluejay said to his elder sister, " Where have all
these people come from ?"   She answered him:
" Do you think that they are people ?   They are
ghosts.   They are ghosts."   Now these people
always spoke in whispers, and Bluejay could
not hear what they said, and did not understand
them.

He stayed a long time with his elder sister.
One day she said to him: " Why do you not
do as they do ?   Go fishing with them, with
your dip-net."   He said, " I will do so."   When
it got dark he made ready to go, and a boy also
made ready.   His sister said: " This is your
brother-in-law's relation.   You two had better
go together.   Do not speak much to him.   Keep
silent."

They put their canoe in the water and started, and as they were paddling down the river
they saw ahead of them some people, also going down the river in a canoe and singing.
When they had almost overtaken them Bluejay began to sing too, joining in their song,
and at once the people were silent.   He looked
back at the boy in the stern of the canoe, but
now there was no boy there, only a pile of

bones. The noise Bluejay made caused the boy to disappear, and only bones were left. Now, as they floated down the stream, Bluejay sat silent, and was wondering what all this meant, and pretty soon when he looked back at the stern of the canoe the boy was sitting there again. Bluejay said to him, speaking slowly and in a low voice, " Where is your fishing-fence ?" The boy answered, " It is beyond here, down the stream." They went on farther; then Bluejay said out loud and suddenly, " Where is your fishing - fence ?" Only bones were in the stern of the canoe. Again Bluejay was silent, and when he next looked back the boy was again in the canoe. Bluejay again spoke to him in low tones, and said, " Where is your fishing-fence ?" The boy answered, " Here."

Now they began to fish, Bluejay using the dip-net, while the boy held the canoe. Soon Bluejay felt something in his net and raised it, but only two dead branches were in it. He threw them out, and again put his net into the water. Again he felt something in it and raised it, and it was full of leaves. He threw them out, but a part of the leaves fell in the canoe,

"THERE WAS NO BOY THERE, ONLY A PILE OF BONES"

Bluejay Visits the Ghosts

and the boy gathered them up. Again he caught
a branch and threw it out into the water; again
he caught some leaves and threw them out, but
a part of them fell in the canoe. The boy
gathered them up. Again he caught two
branches—both large ones. He was pleased
with these branches, and said to himself, " I
will take these back to Ioí; she can use them
to build her fire." At length they turned back
and went homeward and reached the village.
Bluejay was angry because he had caught nothing.

When they went up from the beach to the
houses the boy was carrying a mat full of trout.
After the trout were roasted and the people
were eating them, the boy talked a great deal,
saying: " He threw out of the canoe all that
he had caught. If he had not thrown it away,
our canoe would have been almost full." His
elder sister said to Bluejay, " Why did you
throw away what you had caught?" " I threw
away what I caught because they were
branches," said Bluejay. His sister said: " Do
you think they were branches? That is our
food. When you caught leaves, those were
trout. When you caught branches, those were

39

fall salmon." Bluejay did not believe this.
He said to her: "I brought home to you two
branches. You can use them to make your
fire." His sister went to the beach and found
two fall salmon in the canoe. She took them
up to the house and went in, carrying them in
her hand. Bluejay said to her, "Where did
you steal those fall salmon, Ioí?" She answered, "These are what you caught." Bluejay said to himself, "Ioí keeps telling lies to
me all the time."

When day came Bluejay went down to the
water's edge, to the beach. There on the beach
were the canoes of the ghosts. They were old
and full of holes, and partly grown over with
moss. He went up to the house and said to
his sister, "How bad your husband's canoes are,
Ioí." She answered, "After this keep quiet,
or the people will get tired of you." But he
repeated, "The canoes of these people are full
of holes." She said to him, angrily: "People?
people? They are ghosts."

When it again grew dark Bluejay again made
himself ready, and the boy got ready, and they
went fishing. Now Bluejay teased that boy.
As they were going along he shouted, and only

"ONLY BONES LAY THERE"

Bluejay Visits the Ghosts

bones were in the canoe. He did this several times, but at last they reached the fishing-place, and began to fish with the dip-net. Now Bluejay took into the canoe all the branches that he caught, and all the leaves, and when the tide began to fall their canoe was full, and they started homeward. Now he began to tease the ghosts, and when they met one he shouted, and only bones were in the canoe. At last they reached home, and he carried up to his sister's house part of what he had caught. She also carried up a part — salmon of two kinds.

The next morning when it became day he went through the village again, and he found many bones in those houses.

It got dark, and some one said, " A whale has been found." His elder sister gave him a knife, and said to him, " Quick, run! a whale has been found." Then Bluejay ran fast, and when he reached the beach he met some of those people. He called out to them in a loud voice, asking them, " Where is this whale?" Only bones lay where the people had stood. He kicked the skulls out of the way and ran on a long distance, and met some other people. Again

he called out loudly to them; only bones lay
there. He did this several times. At last he
came to a big log, thrown up on the beach—a
big log with thick bark—and many people were
at work peeling off that bark. Bluejay shouted. Only bones lay there. That bark was
full of pitch. Bluejay began to peel it off.
He peeled off two pieces and put them on his
shoulder and went home. As he was going
along he said to himself, "I thought it was
really a whale, but it is only a fir-tree." He
kept on, and at last he reached the house. Outside the door he threw down the bark and went
in. He said to his elder sister, "I thought
it was really a whale, but you see it is only
bark." His elder sister said to him: "It is
whale, it is whale. Do you think it is bark?"
She went outside, and there two cuts of whale
meat lay on the ground. Ioí said, "It is a good
whale; its blubber is very thick." Bluejay
looked at it. Now he believed that a whale
lay on the beach. He turned back and met a
person who was carrying bark on his back.
Bluejay shouted, and only bones lay there. He
took the piece of bark and put it on his shoulder and carried it home. In this way he treat-

"ITS HEAD WAS SO HEAVY THAT IT THREW IT DOWN

Bluejay Visits the Ghosts

ed all these ghosts, and after a while he had a great deal of whale meat.

Bluejay continued to live there. One day he went into a house in the village and took a child's skull and put it on the bones of a grown-up person. He took the large skull and put it on the child's bones. Thus he did to all these people. When night came the child sat up, intending to rise to its feet, but it fell over. Its head was so heavy that it threw it down. The old man got up. His head was light. The next morning when it became day he changed these heads back again. Sometimes he changed the legs of the ghosts, so that he gave small legs to an old man and large legs to a child. Sometimes he gave a man's legs to a woman, and a woman's legs to a man. After a time the ghosts began to dislike him. Ioí's husband said to her: " These people dislike Bluejay because he treats them in this way. It will be good for you to tell him to go away to his home, for now people do not like him." Ioí tried to stop her younger brother, but he would not listen to her. Now again when it became day Bluejay arose early. Ioí had in her arms a skull. Bluejay threw it away, saying, " Why does she hold

43

The Punishment of the Stingy

that skull in her arms?" She said to him, "Ah! you have broken your brother-in-law's neck." It became night, and his brother-in-law was sick. His relations tried to cure him, and pretty soon the brother-in-law got well.

Now Bluejay started to go to his home. But as he was going home he got caught in a fire, and was burned and died. Then he started back for the country of the ghosts. When he came to the river he called out to his elder sister, and she said, "Ah, my brother is dead."

She put her canoe into the water and went across the river to fetch him. When she reached him he said to her, "Your canoe is pretty, Ioí." She said to him, "You used to say that canoe was grown over with moss." Bluejay thought: "Ioí is always telling lies to me. The other canoes had holes and were moss-covered." She said to him, "You are dead now; that makes the difference." Bluejay thought, "Ioí keeps telling lies to me."

Soon she carried him to the other side of the river, and he saw the people. They were playing games — dice and the ring game — and dancing — *tum, tum, tum, tum* — and singing. Bluejay wanted to go to these singers. He tried

44

Bluejay Visits the Ghosts

to sing and to call out loud, but they laughed
at him. Then he went into his brother-in-law's
house. There sat a chief, a good-looking man;
it was Ioí's husband. Ioí said, "And you
broke his neck." Bluejay thought, "Ioí keeps
telling me lies."

"Where did these canoes come from? They
are pretty." Ioí answered, "And you said
they were moss-grown." Bluejay thought:
"Ioí is always telling lies. The others were
full of holes, and were partly overgrown with
moss." "You are dead now," said his sister;
"that makes the difference."

Then Bluejay gave it up and became
quiet.

The Girl Who Was the Ring

The Girl Who Was the Ring*

Y the bank of a river stood a lodge, in which lived four brothers and their sister. The boys made arrows. To the branch of a tree in front of the lodge they had hung a rawhide strap, such as women use for carrying wood, so as to make a swing for the girl.

Whenever their meat was all gone and they began to get hungry, the girl used to send her brothers into the timber to cut dogwood shoots to make arrows. When the arrows were ready, she would get into the swing and the boys would swing her. As the swing moved, they

* Of all the games played by men among the Pawnee Indians, none was so popular as the stick game. This was an athletic contest between pairs of young men, and tested their fleetness, their eyesight, and their skill in throwing the stick. The implements used were a ring six inches in diameter, made of buffalo rawhide, and two elaborate and highly ornamented slender sticks, one for each player. One of the two contestants rolled the

would see dust rising all around the horizon, and would know that the Buffalo were coming. Then all four boys would take their bows and arrows, and stand about the swing so as to protect the girl and not let the Buffalo come near her. When the Buffalo had come close, the boys would kill them in a circle all about the swing. They would quickly carry the girl into the lodge, and would kill so many Buffalo that the rest would be frightened and run away. So they would have plenty to eat, and the dried meat would be piled high in the lodge.

One day the boys went out to get wood for arrows, and left the girl in the lodge alone. While they were away a Coyote came to the lodge and talked to the girl. He said to her: "Granddaughter, I am very poor, and I am

ring over a smooth prepared course, and when it had been set in motion the players ran after it side by side, each one trying to throw his stick through the ring. This was not often done, but the players constantly hit the ring with their sticks and knocked it down, so that it ceased to roll. The system of counting was by points, and was somewhat complicated, but in general terms it may be said that the player whose stick lay nearest the ring gained one or more points. In this story, the Buffalo by their mysterious power transformed the girl into a ring, which they used in playing the stick game.

THE STICK GAME

The Girl Who Was the Ring

very hungry. I have no meat in my lodge, and my children also are hungry. I told my relations that I was coming to ask you for food, and they have been laughing at me. They said, ' Your granddaughter will not give you anything to eat.' "

The girl answered him: " Grandfather, here is plenty of meat. This house is full of it. Take what you want. Take the fattest pieces. Take it to your children. Let them eat."

The Coyote began to cry. He said: " Yes, my relations laughed at me when I said I was going to visit you and ask you for something to eat. They said you would not give me anything. I do not want any dried meat—I want some fresh meat to take to my children. Have pity on me, and let me put you in the swing, so as to bring the Buffalo. I do not want to swing you hard so as to bring the Buffalo in great herds. I want to swing you only a little so as to bring a few Buffalo. I have a quiver full of arrows to keep the Buffalo off."

The girl said: " No, grandfather, I cannot do this. My brothers are away. Without them we can do nothing."

Then the Coyote slapped his breast and said:

The Punishment of the Stingy

" Look at me. Am I not a man and strong?
I can run around you fast, after you are in
the swing, and I can keep the Buffalo off. I
can shoot clear through a Buffalo. I have
plenty of arrows, and I need only use a single
one for each Buffalo. Come on, I want to
swing you just a little, so that but few Buffalo
will come." So he coaxed the girl, but still
she refused.

After he had begged her for a long time,
she agreed to let him swing her a little, and
got in the swing. He began to swing her, at
first gently, but all at once he pushed her
very hard, and kept doing this until she swung
high. She screamed and cried, and tried to get
off the swing, but it was now too late. All
around—from all sides—the Buffalo were coming in great crowds. The Coyote had made
ready his arrows, and was running around
the girl, trying to kill the Buffalo and
keep them off, but they crowded upon him—
so many that he could do nothing—and at last
he got frightened and ran into the lodge. The
Buffalo were now just all over the ground
about the lodge, and suddenly one of the young
Bulls, the leader of a big band, as he passed

SWINGING THE GIRL TO CALL THE BUFFALO

under the swing, threw up his head, and the girl disappeared, but the Coyote, peeping out of the lodge door, saw on the horn of this Bull a ring, and then he knew that this ring was the girl. Then the Bull ran away fast, and all the Buffalo ran after him.

When the Buffalo had gone, the Coyote came out of the lodge and saw that the girl was not there. He did not know what to do. He was frightened. Pretty soon he heard the girl's brothers coming. They had seen the dust, and knew that some one was swinging their sister, and that the Buffalo had come. They hurried back, running fast, and when they reached the lodge they found the Coyote just dragging himself out of a mud-hole. He crawled out, crying, and pretended that the Buffalo had run over him and trampled him. His bow and arrows were in the mud. He told the brothers his story and said that he had tried hard to save the girl, but that he had not known that so many Buffalo would come. He said he had thought that the girl must be swung high, so that the Buffalo could see her from a long way off.

The brothers felt very sorry that their sis-

The Punishment of the Stingy

ter was lost. They counselled together to see
what they should do, trying to decide what
would be the best plan to get her back again.
While they were talking about this, the Coyote,
with all the mud upon him, stood before them
and said: " Brothers, do not feel sorry because
your sister is lost. I will get her back again.
Live on just as you always do. Do not think
about this. Do not let it trouble you. I will
get her back again." After he had spoken thus,
he said, " Now I am going to start off on the
war-path," and he left them and went away.

He journeyed on alone considering what he
should do, and at length, as he was travelling
along over the prairie, he met a Badger, who
said to him, " Brother, where are you going?"
The Coyote said: " I am going on the war-
path against my enemies. Will you join my
party?" The Badger said, " Yes, I will join
you." They went on. After they had gone a
long way, they saw a Swift Hawk sitting on
the limb of a tree by a ravine. He asked them
where they were going, and they told him, and
asked him if he would go with them. He said
he would go. After a time they met a Kit
Fox, and asked him to join them, and he did

COYOTE HOLDS A COUNCIL OF WAR

so. Then they met a Jack Rabbit, who said he would go with them. They went on, and at length they met a Blackbird, and asked him to join them. He said: " Let it be so. I will go."

Soon after they had all got together they stopped and sat down, and the Coyote told them how the girl had been lost, and said that he intended to try to get her back. Then they talked, and the Coyote told them the plan that he—the leader—had made. The others listened, and said that they would do whatever he told them to do. They were all glad to help to recover the girl.

Then they all stood up and made ready to start, and the Coyote said to the Blackbird, " Friend, you stay here until the time comes." So the Blackbird remained there where they had been talking, and the others went on. After they had gone some distance farther, the Coyote told the Hawk to stop and wait there. He did so. The others went on a long way, and then the Coyote said to the Rabbit, " You stay here." The others went on, and at the next stopping-place he left the Kit Fox; and at the next—last of all—he left the Badger.

The Punishment of the Stingy

Then the Coyote went on alone and travelled a long way, and at length he came to the Buffalo camp. He went out to the place where the young Bulls used to play the stick game, and lay down there. It was early in the morning.

After a time some of the young Bulls came out, and began to roll the ring and to throw their sticks at it. The Coyote now pretended to be very sick. His hair was all covered with mud, and his tongue hung out of his mouth, and he staggered about and fell down and then got up again, and seemed to feel badly. Sometimes he would get over near to where the ring was being rolled, and then the young Bulls would call out: " Here, hold on! Get away there! Don't get in the way."

After a little while the Coyote pretended that he felt better, and he got up and went over to where the young Bulls were sitting, looking on at the game, and sat down with them, and watched the play with the others. Every now and then two of the young Bulls would begin to dispute over the game, each saying that his stick was the nearer to the ring, and sometimes they would wrangle for a long time. Once,

The Girl Who Was the Ring

while they were doing this, the Coyote went up
to them and said: "Here! You men need not
quarrel about this. Let me look. I know all
about this game. I can tell which stick is the
nearer." The Bulls stopped talking and looked
at him, and then said: "Yes, let him look. Let
us hear what he says." Then the Coyote went
up to the ring and looked, and said, pointing:
"That stick is nearest. That man has won."
The Bulls looked at each other, and nodded
their heads and said: "He knows. He is
right." The next time they had a dispute, he
decided it again, and all were satisfied.

At length two of the young Bulls had a very
fierce dispute, and almost came to fighting over
it. The Coyote came up and looked, and said:
"This is very close. I must look carefully,
but I cannot see well if you are all crowding
around me in this way. I must have room.
You would all better go over to that hill, and
sit down there and wait for me to decide."
The Bulls all went over to the hill and sat
down, and then the Coyote began to look. First
he would go to one stick and look carefully,
and then he would go to the other and look.
The sticks were about the same distance from

the ring, and for a long time it seemed that he could not make up his mind which was the nearer. He went backward and forward, looking at the sticks, and stooping down and putting his hands on his knees and squinting, and at last, when once his face was close to the ground, he suddenly snatched up the ring in his mouth, and started, running as hard as he could, for the place where he had left the Badger.

As soon as he had started, all the Bulls on the hill saw what he was doing — that he was taking the ring away from them — and they started after him. They did not want to lose the ring, for it was very useful to them, and they played with it all the time. When the Buffalo in the camp saw that the young Bulls had started, they all followed, so that soon all the Buffalo were rushing after the Coyote. He ran fast, and for a long time he kept ahead of the Buffalo, but they followed, a great mass of Buffalo crowding and pushing, running as hard as they could run. At last the Coyote was beginning to get tired, and was running more slowly, and the Buffalo were beginning to catch up to him, but he was getting near to where the Badger was. After a time

"'I CAN TELL WHICH STICK IS THE NEARER.'"

The Girl Who Was the Ring

the Buffalo were getting nearer to the Coyote.
He was very tired, and it seemed to him as if
he could not run any farther. If he did not
soon get to where he had left the Badger, the
Buffalo would run over him and trample him
to death, and get back the ring. At length,
when they were close behind him, he ran over
the top of a little hill, and down in the valley
below saw the Badger sitting at the mouth of
his hole. The Coyote raced down the hill as
fast as he could, and when he got to the hole
he gave the ring to the Badger, and just as the
herd of Buffalo got to the place, they both
dived down into the hole.

The Buffalo crowded about the Badger's
hole, and began to paw the ground, to dig it
up so as to get the Coyote and the ring, but
the Badger had dug a hole a long way under
the ground, and while the Buffalo were digging
he ran along through this hole and came out
far off, and ran as hard as he could towards
the brothers' lodge. Before he had gone very
far, some of the Buffalo on the outside of the
herd saw him, and called out to the others:
"There he is! There he goes!" Then all the
Buffalo started again and ran after the Badger.

The Punishment of the Stingy

When they had come pretty close to him, he would stop running and dig another hole, and while the Buffalo were crowding around the hole, trying to dig him out, he would dig along under the ground, until he had got far beyond them, and would then come to the top of the ground, and run as fast as he could towards the lodge. Then the Buffalo would see him and follow him.

In this way he went a long distance, but at length he got tired and felt that he could not run or dig much farther. He was almost spent. At last, when he dug out of the ground, he saw not far off the Kit Fox, lying curled upon a rock, asleep in the sun. He called out: " Oh, my brother, I am almost tired out! Help me!" The Kit Fox jumped up and ran to him and took the ring in his mouth and started running, and the Badger dug a deep hole, and stayed there. The little Fox ran fast, gliding along like a bird; and the Buffalo, when they saw him running, chased him and ran hard.

The Kit Fox is a swift animal, and for a long time he kept ahead of the Buffalo. When he was almost tired out, he came to where the Rabbit was, and gave him the ring, and ran

into a hole, and the Rabbit ran on. The Buffalo followed the Rabbit, but he ran fast and
kept ahead of them for a long time. When
they had almost caught him, he came to where
the Hawk was sitting. The Hawk took the
ring in his claws and flew off with it, and the
Rabbit ran off to one side and hid in the long
grass. The Buffalo followed the Hawk, and
ran after him. They seemed never to get
tired. The Hawk, after he had been flying a
long time, began to feel very weary. He
would sail down low over the Buffalo's backs,
and was only just able to keep above them. At
last he got near to where the Blackbird was.

When the Blackbird heard the pounding of
many hoofs and knew that the Buffalo were
coming, he flew up on a sunflower stalk and
waited. When the Buffalo came to the place
where he was, he flew up over them to the
Hawk, and took the ring on his neck, and
flew along over the Buffalo. The ring was
heavy for so small a bird, and he would
alight on the backs of the Buffalo and fly from
one to another. The Buffalo would toss their
heads and try to hit him with their horns, but
he kept flying from one to another, and the

The Punishment of the Stingy

Buffalo behind were always pushing forward to get near the ring, and they pushed the other Buffalo ahead of them. Pretty soon the herd passed over a hill and were rushing down to the place on the river where the brothers' lodge stood.

Ever since their sister had been lost, the brothers had been making arrows, and now they had piles of them stacked up about the lodge. When they saw the Buffalo coming they got their bows and took their arrows in their hands, and shot and shot until they had killed many, many Buffalo, and the rest were frightened and ran away.

The Blackbird had flown into the lodge with the ring, and after the brothers had finished killing, they went into the lodge. And there, sitting by the fire and smiling at them as they came in, they saw their sister.

The First Corn

The First Corn

A LONG time ago there lived in the Pawnee village a young man who was a great gambler. Every day he played at sticks, and he was almost always unlucky. Sometimes he would lose everything that he had, and would even lose things belonging to his father. His father had often scolded him about gambling, and had told him that he ought to stop it. There were two things that he never staked; these two things were his shield and his lance.

One day he played sticks for a long time, and when he got through he had lost everything that he had except these two things. When he went home at night to his father's lodge he told his relations what he had done, and his father said to him: " My son, for a long time you have been doing this, and I have many times spoken

The Punishment of the Stingy

to you about it. Now I have done. I cannot have you here any longer. You cannot live here in my lodge or in this village. You must go away."

The young man thought about it for a little while, and then he said: "Well, I will go. It does not make much difference where I am." So he took his shield and his spear and went out of the lodge and started to go away from the village. When he got outside of the village and had gone some distance, he heard behind him a loud rushing sound like a strong wind—the sound kept getting nearer and louder — and all at once it was above him, and then the sound stopped, and something spoke to him and said: "Well, I am here. I have come to find you. I have been sent, and am here on purpose to get you and take you with me." The voice that spoke to him was the Wind.

The Wind took the young man up and carried him away towards the west. They travelled many days, and passed over broad prairies and then across high mountains and then over high, wide plains and over other mountains until they came to the end of the world, where

66

the sky bends down and touches the ground.
The last thing the young man saw was the gate
through the edge of the sky. A great buffalo
bull stands in this gateway and blocks it up.
He had to move to one side to let the Wind
and the young man pass through.

Every year one hair drops from the hide of
this bull. When all have fallen the end of the
world will come.

After they had passed through this gate they
went on, and it seemed as if they were passing
over a big water. There was nothing to be seen
except the sky and the water. At last they
came to a land. Here were many people—great
crowds of them. The Wind told the young
man, "These are all waiters on the Father."
They went on, and at last came to the Father's
lodge and went in. When they had sat down
the Father spoke to the young man and said
to him: "My son, I have known you for a
long time and have watched you. I wanted to
see you, and that is why I gave you bad luck
at the sticks, and why I sent my Wind to bring
you here. Your people are very hungry now
because they can find no buffalo, but I am going to give you something on which you can

live, even when the buffalo fail." Then he
gave him three little sacks. The first contained squash seed; the second beans, red and
white, and the third corn, white, red, blue, and
yellow.

The Father said: " Tie these sacks to your
shield, and do not lose them. When you get
back to your people give each one some of
the seeds and tell him to put them in the
ground; then they will make more. These
things are good to eat, but the first year do not
let the people eat them; let them put the yield
away, and the next year again put it in the
ground. After that they can eat a part of what
grows, but they must always save some for
seed. So the people will always have something
to eat with their buffalo meat, and something
to depend on if the buffalo fail." The Father
gave him also a buffalo robe, and said to him:
" When you go back, the next day after you
have got there, call all the people together in
your lodge, and give them what is in this robe,
and tell them all these things. Now you can
go back to your people."

The Wind took the young man back. They
travelled a long time, and at last they came to

The First Corn

the Pawnee village. The Wind put the young man down, and he went into his father's lodge and said, "Father, I am here"; but his father did not believe him, and said, "It is not you." He had been gone so long that they had thought him dead. Then he said to his mother, "Mother, I am here," and his mother knew him and was glad that he had returned.

At this time the people had no buffalo. They had scouted far and near and could find none anywhere, and they were all very hungry. The little children cried with hunger. The next day after he got back, the young man sent out an old man to go through the camp and call all the people to come to his father's lodge. When they were there, he opened his robe and spread it out, and it was covered with pieces of fat buffalo meat piled high. The young man gave to each person all he could carry, but while he was handing out the pieces, his father was trying to pull off the robe the hind-quarters of the buffalo and hide them. He was afraid that the young man might give away all the meat, and he wanted to save this for their own lodge. But the young man said: "Father, do not take this away. Do not touch anything. There is enough."

After he had given them the meat he showed them the sacks of seed and told them what they were for, and explained to them that they must not eat any the first year, but that they must always save some to plant, and the people listened. Then he said to them: "I hear that you have no buffalo. Come out to-morrow and I will show you where to go for buffalo." The people wondered where this could be, for they had travelled far in all directions looking for buffalo. The next day they went out as he had told them, and the young man sent two boys to the top of a high hill close to camp, and told them to let him know what they saw from it. When the boys got to the top of the hill, they saw down below them in the hollow a big band of buffalo.

When the people learned that the buffalo were there, they all took their arrows and ran out and chased the buffalo and made a big killing, so that there was plenty in the camp and they made much dried meat. Four days after this he again sent out the boys, and they found buffalo. Now that they had plenty of

The First Corn

meat they stayed in one place, and when spring came the young man put the seed in the ground. When the people first saw these strange plants growing they wondered at them, for they were new and different from anything that they had ever seen growing on the prairie. They liked the color of the young stalks, and the way they tasselled out, and the way the ears formed. They found that besides being pretty to look at they were good to eat, for when the young man had gathered the crop he gave the people a little to taste, so that they might know that the words that he had spoken were true. The rest he kept for seed. Next season he gave all the people seed to plant, and after that they always had these things.

Later, this young man became one of the head men and taught the people many things. He told them that always when they killed buffalo they must bring the fattest and offer them to the Father. He taught them about the sacred bundles, and told them that they must put an ear of corn on the bundles and must keep a piece of fat in the bundles along with the corn, and that both must be kept out of sight. In the fall they should take the ear

The Punishment of the Stingy

of corn out of the bundle and rub the piece of
fat over it.* Thus they would have good crops
and plenty of food.

All these things the people did, and it was a
help to them in their living.

* Cf. *The Story of the Indian*, p. 194, and *The Indians of To-day*, p. 43.

The Star Boy

The Star Boy

ONE hot night in summer two girls climbed up on an arbor in front of an earth lodge to sleep where it was cool. As they lay there before they went to sleep, they were talking about the different stars that they saw in the sky above them, saying how pretty they were. One of the girls saw a bright star, and pointed to it and said: "I like that one best of all. I choose it for mine." After a little while the girls went to sleep.

When this girl that had chosen the star awoke, she was in a strange country, and saw strange people about her. She cried, and wanted to go back to her home, but the man in whose lodge she was told her that he was the star she had said she liked, and that, as she had chosen him, he had taken her for his wife. Finally, she got over feeling badly and was content to stay with him.

Every day when the evening came he would get ready for his journey. He would comb his hair and paint his face red, and then start out to travel. When it was morning he would be back again.

About three years after this the girl had a baby boy. One day after this she went out to dig roots. Her husband had told her not to dig too deep in the ground, and for a long time she was careful, but one day she dug too deep and dug through that ground. There before her was a hole, through which she could look down and see this world below her. She could see a camp, and near it a party of men playing the stick game. They were very small and looked like ants. She looked at them and looked at them for a long time, and then suddenly she felt that she wanted to go back to where she had come from, and wanted again to see her people—the Pawnees.

After she had thought about this for a long time, she went home and asked her husband to bring her a lot of sinews. He brought them to her, and from the sinews she began to make a rope. It took her a long time to make the rope, and in making it she used all the sinews that she had. After she had finished it, she waited until her man had gone out on his journey, and then put her child on her back and went to the hole, carrying the rope of sinew. She took with her also a long stake, and drove it into the ground near the hole. To this stake she tied the rope, and then let it down through the hole. It seemed to her that it did not reach the ground, but she thought that perhaps it reached almost down to it, and she made up her mind that she would try to descend.

All around the hole she dug the earth away so as to make it large enough for her body to pass through. Then she put her child on her back, and let herself slide down by the rope. For a long time she went down, and at last she came to the end of the rope, but it did not nearly reach the ground. That was far below her. She clung to the rope, crying, for she was afraid to let go and no one came to help her, for there was no one near to hear. It was a long way to the camp.

After a time the woman's husband came back to their lodge and found that his wife was gone.

The Punishment of the Stingy

He looked for her everywhere, but could see nothing of her. At last he found the hole that she had dug, and when he looked down through it he saw her there hanging to the rope. Then he was angry. He looked about on the ground for a stone just the size of the hole, and dropped it through, and it fell on the woman's head and killed her, but by his power the Star Man took care of the little child so that when it fell to the ground it was not hurt.

When the woman fell the boy crawled out from under her. He stayed there by his mother three days. Every now and then he would start to go off somewhere, and would go a little way, and then would come back to his mother and try to rouse her; but she was dead. The fourth day he started to go off a long way, and as he was going along he came to a patch of corn and squashes, and he walked among the corn and pulled some ears and ate them.

Near by this field was a poor little lodge, in which lived an old woman and her little grandson. One day the little boy went into the corn patch and saw there the footprints of a little child. He went back home and told his grandmother about it. They did not know whether

The Star Boy

the tracks had been made by a girl or a boy. They looked for the child everywhere, but could not find it.

At last the old woman told her grandson to take out a flesher and a hoe and leave them in the field. "If it is a girl," the old woman said, "she will take them." The little boy did as she had said, and left the things there, but when the strange child came he did not take them. They could see his tracks where he had walked straight by them. Then the old woman said: "My son, take your bow and arrows and put them there. If it is a boy he will take them." He did so.

When the little boy next went back to the corn patch after leaving the bow and arrows, they were gone. Then the little boy went into the corn and hid himself and waited. He stayed hidden there until the little Star Boy came back; then he walked up to him. He said: "Come, let us go to where my grandmother lives. We can play there together with our bows and arrows." The boys went to the lodge and went in and ate together. Then they went out and played with their bows and arrows.

They lived thus for a long time. When they

had grown so that they could go a long way from home, they would sometimes stay away too long, and the old woman would get frightened about them and would scold them when they came back.

One day she said to the boys: " My sons, you must never go over there to that place where the timber grows thick. Never go there. That is where your fathers, mothers, uncles, aunts, and brothers were killed by a grizzly bear. It is dangerous to go there."

Not long after that the little Star Boy said, " Let us go out and kill little birds." They went out, and when they had got some distance from the lodge he said, " Brother, let us go over to that place where grandmother told us not to go." The other boy said: " It is good. We will go." They went over there, and when they had gone into the thick timber, suddenly they saw a bear. It seemed very angry and roared and growled. The Star Boy laughed at it, and walked up to it and tapped it on the head with his bow. His father was using his power so that the bear could not hurt him. The boy took the bear home with him to the lodge, and called to his grandmother to come

out and said, "Grandmother, here is a bear;
you can have him to pack wood and water for
you." The old woman was scared. The boy
killed the bear with his little arrows.

One day after that the old woman said to
the boys: "Now, boys, do not go to that thick-
timbered place over there. That is where some
of your brothers and relations disappeared. Do
not go there." Soon after this, one day when
they were out hunting little birds and had got
away from the lodge, the Star Boy said, "Brother, let us go over to that place where grandmother told us not to go. Let us see what is
there." They went, and as they were going
along through the timber they saw a panther.
The panther growled and looked very fierce,
but the boy walked up to it and shot his little
arrow at it and killed it. His father was help-
ing him. The boys skinned it and took it home
and stuffed it with grass and stood it up in the
lodge. Their grandmother was away. When
she came back they told her to go into the
lodge; they said, "We have something nice for
you in there." She went into the lodge, and
when she saw the panther she was frightened
almost to death, and the boys laughed. The

The Punishment of the Stingy

boys said to the old woman, " Grandmother, we have done this so that we could put this skin outside the lodge to scare away other animals so that they will not come near us."

The grandmother said: " Boys, boys, you must not do as you have been doing. You must not go so far away, and you must not go into danger. Right up there on the hill is a den of snakes. I do not want you to go there. You must not go near that place." Soon after this the Star Boy said to his playmate: " Brother, let us go over to that hill where the snakes live. Let us each take a piece of rock and we will kill them." They went, and when they got to the place he said: " Sit down. Put your rock on the ground and sit down on it. I know what the snakes are going to do, but our father will take care of us."

The snakes came out of the den—great lots of them—and came towards the boys. All at once the boys saw a cloud rising and coming towards them, and pretty soon it began to rain where the snakes were, and the water got so deep that the snakes were swimming, but where the boys were it did not rain. On them the sun was shining warm and bright. Then the sun got hotter and hotter, and at last it was so hot it made the water boil and killed all the snakes.

The boys went home, and the old woman's grandson told her what had happened—just how it all was. Then she said to him: "Grandson, I believe there is power in this little boy. Now we will go back to our people." They had left their people because they were poor and had no horses, and the others in the camp did not take care of them. She said, "We will go back and try to find out where this boy came from, and whether he is a relative of any of our people there." Before they started the grandmother asked the Star Boy where he came from. He told her that he did not know; that he had come from above, but he remembered that his mother had told him that they did not belong up there, but down below, and that she had been taken up by a star. He said that she had come down with him on her back, but had been killed by a stone dropped from above, which had hit her on the head but did not kill him.

Then the old woman remembered that once a girl had disappeared one night from the camp when she was sleeping on an arbor, and that this girl was the daughter of a chief.

They left their lodge and went back to their people. When they reached the camp, they had a lodge of their own and all lived together. His relations, when they found out who the Star Boy was, wanted him to come and live with them, but for a long time he would not do so. When he did go, he took the old woman and her grandson with him.

When he grew up he began to go on the warpath, and he had good luck and struck many of his enemies. At length he married the daughter of a chief, and the grandson married another daughter.

The Grizzly Bear's Medicine

The Grizzly Bear's Medicine

A LONG time ago there lived in a camp of Pawnees a certain poor boy. His father had only one pony. Once he had been a leading man in the tribe, but now he seemed to be unlucky. When he went on the war-path he brought back nothing, and when he fought he did nothing, and the people did not now look up to him.

There was a chief's son who loved the poor boy, and these two went together all the time. They were like brothers; they used to hunt together and go courting together, and when they were travelling, the poor boy often rode one of the ponies of the chief's son, and the latter used to go to the poor boy's lodge and sleep there with him.

Once the camp went off to hunt buffalo, and the poor boy and the chief's son rode together all the time. After the people had made camp

87

The Punishment of the Stingy

at a certain place, the chiefs decided to stop here for four days, because the buffalo were close by, and they could kill plenty and dry the meat here. North of the camp was a hill on which grew many cedar-trees, and during the day the poor boy had overheard people saying that many Indians had been killed on that hill, among those trees. They said that no one ought to go there, for it was a dangerous place.

That night the chief's son went over to his friend's lodge to sleep there, but before they went to bed he left the lodge for a time, and while he was gone the poor boy, as he sat there waiting, began to think about himself and how unhappy he was. He remembered how poor he and his father were, and how everybody looked down on them and despised them, and it did not seem to him that things would ever be any better for them than they were now. For a long time he sat there thinking about all these things, and the more he thought of them the worse they seemed, and at last he felt that he was no longer glad to live, and he made up his mind to go up into those cedars.

He went out of the lodge and started to go

The Grizzly Bear's Medicine

up towards the trees. It was bright moonlight, so that he could see well. Just before he reached the edge of the timber he crossed a ravine, and saw there many skeletons of people who had been killed. The ground was white with these bones. He went on into the cedars, and came to a ravine leading up the hill and followed it. As he went on he saw before him a trail and followed it, and when he came to the head of the ravine there was a big hole in the bank, and the trail led to it. He stopped for a moment when he came to this hole, but then he went in, and when he had entered he saw there, sitting by the fire, a big she-bear and some little cubs.

As the boy stood there looking at her, the she-bear said to him: "I am sorry that you have come here. My husband is the one who kills persons and brings them here for the children and me to eat. You had better go back to your people quickly, or he will eat you up. He has gone hunting, but he will soon be back again. If he finds you here he will kill you."

The poor boy said: "Well, I came here on purpose to be killed, and I give myself up to you. I shall be glad to be eaten by you. I

The Punishment of the Stingy

am here ready to be killed. I am yours. Take
me."

The she-bear said: "Oh, I wish I could do
something to save you, but I cannot. He is
one of those bad bears—a grizzly—medicine.
I can do nothing for you, but I will try. As
soon as you hear any noise outside—any one
coming—pick up that cub, the littlest one, and
hold it in your arms. When he comes in he
will tell you to put it down, but do not do so.
Hold it tight; he loves that one best of all."

All at once the boy heard outside the cave
the noise of a bear snorting and grunting. The
she-bear said, "Pick up the cub, quick; he is
coming." The boy caught up the little bear,
and held it tight to his breast. All at once the
noise came to the mouth of the den and stopped.
It was the Bear. The boy could hear him talking. He said: "Here! somebody has been
about my house. I smell human beings. Yes,
he even came in. Where is he? Let me see
him, so that I may jump upon him and kill
him." When he came in he saw the boy, and
seemed very angry. He stood up on his hind
feet and threw up his hands, and then came
down again and struck his paws on the ground,

90

The Grizzly Bear's Medicine

and then rose up and snorted "*whoof,*" and blew out red dust from his nostrils, and then came down and jumped about, and sometimes sprang towards the boy, as though he were going to seize him. He was very terrible, and the boy was very much afraid.

The Bear called out to the boy in a loud voice: "How dare you take up my child and hold it? Let it go, or I will tear you to pieces and eat you." But the boy still held the cub. No matter what the Bear said or what he did, the boy held fast to the cub.

When the Bear saw that the boy would not let the cub go, he became quiet, and no longer seemed angry. He said: "Boy, you are my son. Put down your brother, for now he is your brother. He shall go with you, he shall be your companion, and shall be with you always as your guide and helper. He has told me your story, and how you are poor, unhappy, and now he has kept you from being eaten up. I have taken pity on you, and we will send you back to your people, where you may do some good among them. My son, I am at the head of all these animal lodges, down at Pahŭk' and at Pahūr' and everywhere else. I am at the head; there is no animal living that is stronger than I; none that I cannot kill. If a man shoots at me, I make the arrow to fall from my skin without hurting me. Look up around my lodge. See these arrows, these guns, these leggings, these beads, and the medicine that men have brought, thinking to kill me; but I have killed them, and have taken these things, and keep them here.

"I knew that your people were coming to this place to hunt. I drove the buffalo over, so that the people should stop here and hunt and kill meat, in order that you might come to my lodge. I know all your feelings. I know that you are sorry for your poor father, my brother, and I wished you to come here, so that I might make you my son and give my power to you, so that you may become a great man among your people. I know that they are now killing buffalo, and that they will be camped here for four days.

"Now, my son, set your brother free. All the power that I have I give to you. I shall kill my son, your little brother there, and give you his skin to keep and to carry away with you, so that he may be your companion and

"SNORTED 'WHOOF,' AND BLEW RED DUST FROM HIS NOSTRILS"

The Grizzly Bear's Medicine

may be with you always. Your brother, your
friend at the camp, is looking for you, mourn-
ing for you, for he thinks you dead, but to-morrow night you shall see him, and shall tell him
to rejoice for you and not to mourn. You shall
tell him where you have been."

The little bear that he was holding said to
the boy: "It is all right now, brother; put me
down. My father means what he says. I am
glad that I am going to be with you, my brother." The boy put him down.

Then the Bear said to his wife: "Get up.
Take that gun." The she-bear took the gun,
and they walked around the fireplace in a circle, and sang, and the boy looked on. The Bear
took the gun and told the boy to look at them,
and to watch carefully everything that they
did. After a little he stopped, and shot his
wife, and she fell down dead. Then he put
down the gun, and went to the she-bear and put
his mouth on the wound, and breathed on it
and snorted "*whoof,*" and sucked in his breath
and took the bullet out, and went around the
lodge, singing and making motions, and then
he took hold of the she-bear and lifted her to
her feet, and supported her, and pushed her

93

around, and helped her, and at last she walked, and was well. Then he called the boy to him and said, " Now I will do the same thing to you." And he did the same thing to the boy, and brought him to life in the same way. Then he said, " That is one power I give you to-night."

Then he gave the gun to the boy and went to the other side of the lodge, and sat up, and said, " Now I will open my mouth, and you shoot me right in the mouth." He opened his mouth, and the boy shot him, and he fell over. After a moment he got up on his feet and slapped his paws on his chest several times, and the bullet came out of his mouth, and he walked around the fireplace two or three times, and made motions and grunted, and then he was well. Then he took the boy in his arms, and hugged him and kissed him and breathed on him, and said : " Now I give you my power. Go over there and I will shoot you as you shot me. Do just as I did." The boy went over there, and the Bear shot him, and the boy did just as the Bear had done, and made himself well.

The Bear then put an arrow in the gun and

shot it at the boy, and when the smoke cleared away the boy found the arrow fast in his throat, the feather end sticking out. The Bear took it out and made him well, and gave him also this power. Then the Bear told him to load the gun with a ball and to shoot it at him, and he did so, and shot the Bear, but the lead was made flat and dropped to the ground. The bullet did not go into the Bear.

The Bear now told the boy to take the bow and arrow and to shoot at him with all his strength. The boy did this, but the arrow did not go through the Bear, but the spike rolled up and the shaft was split. The Bear said: " Now you see, my son, that the gun and the bow, the bullet and the arrow, cannot harm me. You shall have the same power. When you go into battle you shall not carry a gun nor arrows, for they are not mine, but you shall take this paint, and put it all over your body, then put this feather on your head, and take this club, which is part of my jawbone. All these things have my power and medicine. When you are carrying these things your enemy cannot hurt you, even if you run right on to him; but with one stroke of this club you shall kill your enemy."

The next morning the Bear took the boy out on the prairie and showed him the different roots and leaves of medicines, and told him how to use them; how he should eat some medicine and then he could cure the wounded by just breathing on the wound.

That night the Bear said to him: "Hereafter you shall have the same feelings as the bear. When you get angry, you will have a grunt like a bear; and if you get too fierce, tushes like a bear's will stick out of your mouth, so that the people will know that you are very angry. You shall have my power, and you can go into any of the lodges of the animals, of which I am the chief." And he told him how to get into these lodges.

That day they stayed in the Bear's lodge, and the Bear took the claw off from his little finger and gave it and a little bundle of medicine to the boy. He said, "Take this claw and this bundle of medicine and put them on a string and wear them on your neck always, the claw hanging in front." He taught him how to make plums grow on trees, and how to make ground - cherries come out of his mouth.

That night he sent the boy back to the camp. He said: " Tell your father and mother not to mourn for you, for you will return in two days more. I have driven plenty of buffalo to this place, and the people will kill them and dry the meat. Now go to the camp and get a pipe and some tobacco, and bring them here."

The boy went back to the camp. When he went into the lodge his father and mother were glad to see him. He told them not to be anxious about him, and not to say anything about his having been away. Then he went out and found his brother, the chief's son, asleep. He said to him: "Wake up, brother. I want you to get some tobacco and a pipe from your father. Tell no one that it is for me. Bring it here. I want to smoke with you. I am going away again, but you must stay in camp. I shall return in a few days." The chief's son got the things and gave them to the boy. He wanted to go with him, but the poor boy would not let him.

That same night the boy went back to the Bear's den, carrying with him the pipe and to-

The Punishment of the Stingy

bacco. After he went into the lodge he filled his pipe and lighted it, and he and the Bear smoked together. The Bear said to him: "After you have gone home, whenever you smoke, always point your pipe towards my den and ask me to smoke with you. After lighting your pipe, point it first to Atíus Tiráwat, and then blow a few whiffs to me. Then I shall know that you still remember me. All my power comes from Atíus. He made me. There will be an end to my days as there is to those of every mortal. So long as I live I shall protect you; when I die of old age, you shall die too."

After this he said, "Now bring my youngest boy here." The boy brought the little cub, and the Bear said, "Now kill him." The boy hesitated to do this. He did not want to kill the little bear, but it said to him: "Go on, my brother, kill me. After this I am going to be a spirit, and always to be with you." Then the boy killed him, and skinned him, and tanned his hide. After it was tanned he put some red medicine paint on the hide. When this was done the Bear told him to put his paint, his feather, and his war-club in this hide, and to wrap them up and make a bundle

98

of them. Then he said: "Now, my son, go to your people, and when you get home hang your bundle up at the back of the lodge, and let the people know nothing of all this. Keep it secret. Wherever you go, or wherever you are, I shall be with you."

The boy went home to the camp, and told his mother to hang up his bundle, as the Bear had said. Next morning he was in camp and all the people saw him. They were surprised, for they had thought that he had been killed. By this time the Pawnees had all the buffalo they wanted, and the next day they started back to their village.

After they had reached their home, the boy told the chief's son that he wanted him to go off with him on the war-path. His brother said: "It is good. I will go." The poor boy took his bundle, and they started. After travelling many days they came to a camp of the enemy. They went into the village in the daytime, and took many horses and started away with them, riding hard. Soon the enemy pursued them, and at length they could see them coming, and it seemed as if they must soon overtake them. Then the poor boy got off his horse and stopped, telling his brother to go on, driving the horses.

The boy had painted himself red over his whole body. He held his war-club in his hand, and had his feather tied on his head and the little bear-skin on his back. The enemy soon came up and tried to kill him, but they could not. He would run after one and kill him, and all the others would shoot at him with their arrows, but they could not hurt him, and at last they left him and went back, and he went on and overtook the chief's son. Then his brother saw that he had great power. After this they travelled on slowly, and at last reached the village. His brother told the people that this man was powerful, that they had taken the horses in broad daylight, and the young man had stayed behind on foot and fought the enemy off, while he drove on the horses.

A few days after they reached home, a war-party of the enemy attacked the village. All the Pawnees went out to fight them, but the poor boy stayed behind in the lodge. He took down his bundle, filled the pipe, and pointed it first to Atíus, and then towards the Bear's lodge, and smoked. Then he took the paint and

"THEY COULD NOT HURT HIM"

The Grizzly Bear's Medicine

mixed it with grease, and rubbed it all over his body except his face: that he painted black. Then he put the feather on his head and the little bear-robe on his back, and took his war-club in his hand and started out. The Bear had told him that in going into battle he must never start towards the east, but must attack going towards the west. So he went around, and came on the battle-field from one side.

As he came up he saw that his people were having a hard time, and were being driven back. There was one of the enemy who seemed to be the bravest of all. The poor boy rushed at this man and killed him with his club, and then ran back to his own line. When his people looked at him, and saw that it was really the poor boy who had just done so brave a deed, they knew that what the chief's son had said was true. When he started again to rush towards the enemy's line, all the Pawnees followed him. He ran among the enemy, and with his club killed one here and one there, and the enemy became afraid and ran, and the Pawnees followed and killed many of them. That night they returned to the village, rejoicing over the victory. Everybody was praising the young

101

The Punishment of the Stingy

man. Old men were calling his name, young women were singing about him, and old women dancing before him. People no longer made fun of his father or mother, or of him. Now they looked upon him as a great and powerful person.

The Bear had told him that when he wanted his name changed he must call himself Ku ruks la war' uks ti, Medicine Bear.

That night the Bear came to the boy in his sleep and spoke to him. He said: "My son, to-morrow the chief of the tribe is going to ask you to take his daughter for your wife, but you must not do this yet. I wish you to wait until you have done certain things. If you take a wife before that time, your power will go from you."

The next day the chief came to Medicine Bear and asked him to marry his daughter, and told him the people wanted him to be their head chief. He refused.

Some time after this all the different tribes that had been attacked by them joined forces and came down together to fight the Pawnees. All the people went out to meet them, but he stayed in his lodge and painted himself, and put

The Grizzly Bear's Medicine

his feather in his head and the bear-claw on his neck and his bear-skin on his back, and smoked as he always did, and took his club and went out. When he came to the battle, the Pawnees were having a hard time, because the enemy were so many. Medicine Bear charged, and killed a man, and then came back, and the second time he charged, the people charged all together, following him, and they killed many and drove the enemy off, and those who had the fastest horses were the only ones who got away. The Pawnees went home to the village. Everybody rejoiced, and there were many scalp-dances. Now the poor boy was more highly thought of than ever. Even the chiefs bowed their heads when they saw him. They could not equal him. This time he called himself Ku ruks ti carish, Angry Bear.

After the excitement had quieted down, one day the head chief said: "Medicine Bear, in all this tribe there is no chief who is equal to you. Sit down by my daughter. Take her for your wife, and take my place as chief. I and my wife will go out of this lodge, and it shall be yours. You shall be the chief of the tribe.

The Punishment of the Stingy

Whatever you say we will abide by." The poor boy said: "My father, I will think about this. By morning I will let you know." In the night, before he slept, he filled the pipe and smoked as the Bear had told him to do, and then he went to bed. In dreams the Bear said to him: "My son, you have done what I wished you to do. Now the power will remain with you as long as you shall live. Now you can marry, if you will."

But the boy was not yet ready to do this. The girl was very pretty, and he liked her, but he felt that before he married there were still some things that he must do. He called his brother and said to him, "Go, kill the fattest of the buffalo; bring it to me, and I will take a long journey with you."

His brother went hunting and killed a buffalo, and brought the meat home, and they dried it and made a bundle of it. Medicine Bear told his brother to carry this bundle and a rawhide rope and a little hatchet, and they started on a journey towards the Missouri River. One day towards evening they reached the river, and they found themselves on top of a steep-cut bluff. The river ran at its foot. The poor

The Grizzly Bear's Medicine

boy cut a cottonwood pole and drove it into the ground, and tied the rope to it, and then tied the other end of the rope about his brother's body. Then he sharpened a stick and gave it to his brother and said: " Now take the bundle of meat, and I will let you down over the bank. You must put the meat on a ledge of the cliff, and when the birds come you must feed them. Give a piece to the first one that comes, and then take your sharp stick and get another piece, and so feed all the birds. They are the ones that have power, and they can take pity on you." So he let the chief's son down.

The first bird that came was a buzzard, then an eagle, then hawks and owls, all kinds of birds that kill their prey. He fed them all. While he was doing this, the poor boy was above lying on top of the bank. Late in the afternoon, just as the sun was going down, he saw, far up the river, what looked like a flock of geese coming. They came nearer and nearer, and at last passed out of sight under the bank. Afterwards, when he looked down on the river, he could see in the water red light as if it were all on fire, and as he lay on the bank he could

105

The Punishment of the Stingy

hear down below him the sound of drumming and singing just as plain as could be, and all the time the chief's son was hanging there in front of the bank, and the poor boy would call down to him to cry and ask the animals to take pity on him. When Medicine Bear had done this, he started back and went home, leaving the chief's son hanging there.

The chief's son stayed there all the night and all the next day, and for three days and nights, and on the night of the fourth day he fell asleep. When he awoke he was in a lodge. It was under the Missouri River. When he looked about him he saw that those in the lodge were all animals. There was the beaver, there was the otter, two buffalo, the antelope, hawks, owls, ermines, bears, frogs, woodpeckers, catfish—all kinds of animals. On each side of the lodge was a little pool, and in each pool sat a goose, and every time they sang, the geese would shake their wings on the water, and it sounded just like drumming. The chief of the animals spoke to him, saying: "My son, at this time we can do nothing for you. We must first send our messenger up to the Bear's lodge to ask him what we may do for you." While

106

THE CONFERENCE IN THE LODGE

The Grizzly Bear's Medicine

he was saying this the Bear's servant entered the lodge and said: " My father, it is all right. Our father the Bear told me to say to you that his son has sent this young man to you, and you must exert all your power for him."

Now the animals began to make ready to use their power to help the chief's son. First the Beaver talked to the young man, to tell him of his powers and his ways, so that he might perform wonderful acts. How he should take the branch of a tree and strike a man with its point and it would go through him, and then how to draw it out and to make the man well again. He gave him the power to do this. He taught him how to take a stick two feet long and swallow it, and then take it out again from his throat, and gave him this power.

The Otter gave him the power, if his enemies ever attacked him, to break their arrows with his teeth and shoot back the shaft without a spike, and if he hit an enemy with the shaft, it would kill him. " The poison from your mouth will kill him," he said.

The Ground-dog said: " My son, here is my little one. I give him to you. Take him, and if you have an enemy among the doctors in your tribe, take this little one down to the water early in the morning and dip his nose in the water, and when you take it out it will have a piece of liver in its mouth. The man who has tried to kill you will be found dead."

The Owl said: "My son, I give you power to see in the night. When you go on the war-path and want to take horses, the night will be like daytime for you."

The Hawk said: "My son, I give you power to run swiftly, and I give you my war-club, which is my wing. You shall strike your enemy with it only once, and the blow shall kill him. Take also this little black rope; you shall use it when you go on the war-path to catch horses. Take also this scalp which you see hanging down from my claw. You shall be a great man for scalping."

Each of the other animals gave him all his kinds of power.

For two days and two nights they taught him the different kinds of power, and for two days and two nights they taught him the different kinds of roots and herbs for healing the sick. They said to him: "You shall be the great doctor of your people. Every now and

The Grizzly Bear's Medicine

then you must bring us tobacco, so that we can smoke." They further told him that at this time they could teach him only a little, but that afterwards, one at a time, they would meet him out on the prairie, and would teach him more. At last they said: " Now it is time for you to go. Your friend has come, and is waiting for you out on the prairie."

The Buffalo now stood up and said: " My son, I want to be with you always. I give you my robe. Wear it wherever you go, that the people may know that you come from this place." All the animals said, " We want to be with you too." Each one of the birds took off a feather and put it on the robe, and each animal put one of its claws on it, and some put medicine on it. In one of the holes the Beaver tied a little sweet-grass, and others did the same. By the time they were through, the robe was all covered with feathers and claws and smelled sweet. The animals had put their medicine on it so that it smelled sweet. Then the animals said, " Go, my son, to your people, and bring us something to smoke, so that we may be satisfied."

Presently the chief's son found himself upon

the bluff, facing his brother. His brother grasped him in his arms and said: "Oh, my brother, you smell nice. What a fine robe you have on! Look at all these feathers." They hugged each other. Then they went home together. The chief's son had a bundle that the animals had given him.

Soon after this the Pawnees had a big doctors' dance. These boys went into the doctors' lodge and said: "Doctors, you are the head doctors, but we have come to-night to visit you. We want to do a few things ourselves." The doctors all said "*Lau-a*." The young men took seats close to the door, which is the most important place in this dance. All the doctors were surprised, and said "*Uh!*"

The Bear boy got up first and began shooting at the chief's son, just as he had done with the Bear, and all the doctors thought he was powerful, shooting at this young man and curing him. When he got through, it was the other boy's turn. He would take a long sharp stick and thrust it through his brother, and then heal him again, and then take a knife and stab him, and then cure him. He did some powerful things, more so than his brother had

110

done. After the doctors had seen all these things they all said, "Let us have these two for our head doctors." But the poor boy said: "Not so. This one who is sitting by me has more power than I have. He ought to be the head doctor, for I am a warrior, and can never stay in the camp to doctor people. My brother has gone into the animals' lodge, and they have given him more power than I possess." So the chief's son was chosen to be the head doctor.

When the doctors' dance was over, the two brothers at once started to go to the animals' lodge, carrying with them tobacco and a pipe. When they got there, the chief's son told his brother to wait on the bank, that he was going down to take the tobacco and the pipe to his fathers. He jumped off the steep bank into the river, down into the door of the lodge, and went in. When they saw him all the animals slapped their mouths and called out. They were glad to see him. After smoking with them, he went back to his friend. After that the chief's son would go off by himself and would meet the animals on the hills. They would tell him about different roots, and how to doctor this disease and that. He would come back with some roots and herbs and put them away.

Finally the head chief sent for the Bear man and said to him: "My son, I offered you my lodge, my daughter, and the whole tribe. Now take all this. Let me go out of this lodge and look for another one, and you stay here with my daughter." The young man said: "What of my brother? Send for the other chief. Let him give his daughter, his lodge, his people, to him, and this day we will accept your gifts to us. My brother will after this be the head doctor of this tribe." The other chief, when asked to do this, agreed, and it was so done.

The Bear man went often on the war-path, but his brother stayed at home, and fought against the enemy only when they attacked the village. He took charge of the doctors' lodge. The Bear man after this had some children, and when they had grown up he told his son the secrets of his power. He was now beginning to grow old, and his son went on the war-path, while he stayed at home.

One night he had a dream about his father the Bear. The Bear said to him: "My son, I made you great and powerful among your people. The hairs of my body are falling, and soon I shall die. Then you too will die. Tell your son all the secret powers that I gave you. He shall keep the same power that you have had."

Soon after this the old Bear must have died, for the man died. Before he died he said to his brother: "Do not mourn for me, for I shall always be near you. Take care of your people. Cure them when they are sick, and always be their chief."

When the enemy came and attacked the people and wounded any, the chief's son was always there and always cured them. He was a great doctor. At last he also died, but his son had the same kind of power. But these two sons never had so great powers as their fathers.

H

The First Medicine Lodge

The First Medicine Lodge

A GREAT many winters ago the Piegans were camped near a small creek. Their lodges were arranged in a circle, enclosing a large open space. This was long before they had horses. They used dogs to pack with.

The head chief had a daughter. She was good and beautiful. Many young men had asked to marry her, but she had refused them all. One day she went to the stream for water. There she met a boy, well known through the camp, because of a great scar on his cheek, which made him very ugly. From this the people called him Scarface. He was very poor. His mother and father were dead, and he lived with his grandmother. His clothes were old and torn, and he wore about him part of a worn buffalo robe. Yet, though his clothes were poor and his face was ugly, his heart was good, and the

117

The Punishment of the Stingy

cruel taunts of his people often made him very sad.

When Scarface met the beautiful girl, he asked her if she would marry him. She looked at him in scorn and said: "Do you think I would marry such an ugly person as you? When you remove that great scar from your face, come and ask me." Then she left him. He sat for a long time thinking over the cruel words the girl had spoken. His heart was sad. At last he went slowly to his grandmother's lodge.

When he entered he said: "Grandmother, make me some moccasins and put some dried buffalo meat in a sack for me. I am going away and may be gone a long time." She gave him the things he asked for, and he left the lodge and started to go to a butte not far from the camp.

When he reached the top of the butte, he threw himself upon the ground and wept and prayed to the Sun to have pity on him and remove the scar. At last he stood up and made a bed of the stones which he found on the side of the butte. Then he lay down to sleep. While he slept a voice said to him: "My son, rise, and go to the butte to the right of you. There

The First Medicine Lodge

you will find your father." He did as the voice had said.

When he reached the place, he threw himself on the ground and wept as before, and prayed the Sun to help him. He made a bed of stones like the one he had lain on before, and while he slept another voice said: "My son, your journey is not yet ended. Rise and go to that butte still farther to the right. There you will find one who will direct you on your way." Again he obeyed the voice.

When he reached this butte he made his bed as before, and slept, but no voice spoke to him. In the morning he awoke. As he sat on the ground, he was wondering what he should do next. Again a voice spoke, saying, "My friend, shut your eyes." He did so, and in a short time the strange voice said, "Open your eyes and look about you."

When he opened his eyes, he was far up in the blue sky, in another world. It was all a wide prairie. There were no mountains, no trees. There were only rivers, with a few bushes upon their banks. He could now see the person who had spoken to him. He was a young man about his own age, but he was very handsome.

The Punishment of the Stingy

He wore a shirt, leggings, and robe of some
strange animal's fur, and his moccasins were
embroidered in strange and beautiful colors and
patterns. The young man said to Scarface:
"My name is Sun Dog. The Sun is my father
and the Moon my mother. Yonder is my father's
lodge. Let us go to it. My father is not now
there. At night he will enter."

They reached the lodge. Very large it was
and very beautiful. Many unknown animals
were painted on it, and behind it, hanging from
a tripod, were the war clothes of the Sun, made
of the skins of strange animals, and trimmed
with fine feathers. Scarface was ashamed to
enter this beautiful lodge, for his clothes were
poor and his moccasins were worn with travel;
but Sun Dog said to him, "Enter, my new
friend, and fear nothing."

They entered. All about were seats covered
with white robes, and everything was strange.
The Moon was there. Sun Dog approached her
and said: "Mother, I have brought a young
man to our lodge who is very poor. I beg you
to have pity on him and help him in his
trouble." The Moon spoke kindly to Scarface,
and gave him something to eat.

The First Medicine Lodge

When it was time for the Sun to come home, Sun Dog hid Scarface and covered him up with robes. When the Sun came to the door, he stopped and said, " There is a person here." " Yes, father," said Sun Dog, " a good young man, who is in trouble, has come to see you." The Sun said, " Bring him to me." Sun Dog removed the robes and brought Scarface before the Sun. The Sun looked at Scarface a short time, and turning to the Moon, bade her make Scarface as handsome as their own son, and give him some nice clothes to wear. The Moon made some medicine and rubbed it over Scarface. In a short time he was changed into a very handsome young man. The Moon took Sun Dog and Scarface before the Sun and said, " O Sun, tell me which is Sun Dog." The Sun looked at the two boys for a moment, and then pointed to Sun Dog, and said, " This is our son." Again the Moon rubbed the medicine on Scarface, until she was sure that the two young men looked alike, and again she took them before the Sun and said, " O Sun, tell me now which is our son." He looked at them a long time, and, pointing to Scarface, said, " This must be our son."

The Punishment of the Stingy

In the morning before leaving the lodge, the Sun called the young men to him and said, " My children, do not go near that lodge by the river, for in it live four large white birds with long bills with which they pluck out people's hearts. I have had four other sons, but they have all been killed by these birds." Then he left them.

The two young men went out hunting. They went on and on, when suddenly Sun Dog cried out, " This is the place where my brothers were killed! See! there are the birds coming one after another towards us. Let us make haste to get away." He ran away, but Scarface waited until the birds came near him. As they came up, he struck each on the head with a club which he carried, and killed them. After some time Sun Dog returned, and the young men took the birds home to the lodge.

The Moon was very happy when she saw that the destroyers of her sons were dead. When the Sun returned in the evening, Sun Dog said, " Father, my friend killed the bad birds to-day," and he showed them to him. The Sun called Scarface to him and dressed him in clothes made of white buffalo skins and painted

The First Medicine Lodge

his face and said: " It is now time, my son, for you to return to your people, for they need your help. They are beneath us, and not far from here. Sun Dog will take you and will tell you what I wish you to do." After shaking hands with the Sun and Moon, the two young men started on their journey.

After they had gone some distance, they stopped. Sun Dog said: " Soon we will have to part, but first I must tell you what the Sun has commanded you to do. If there are any sick or dying among your people, in order to make them well you must build the Medicine Lodge. First you must get one hundred buffalo tongues. Select four pure women of your tribe to help. Let one woman make the medicine, another cut thin and dry the tongues, and the other two boil the tongues. Go into the tall brush and clear a place for the Medicine Lodge. When everything is ready, call the people together to take part in the dance. Let each take a piece of the tongue, and let all say together, ' Great Sun, let us eat together, and grant to us that our people may recover.' If the women you select to make the medicine and to cut and boil the tongue are pure women, the sick and the dying among your people will recover; if not, they will die.

"Now, my brother," continued Sun Dog, "you have heard the commands of the Sun. You will soon find yourself on the butte you came from. We must now part." They shook hands. Sun Dog said, "Shut your eyes." Scarface shut his eyes, and when he opened them he found himself sitting at the foot of the butte from which he came. The circular camp lay before him.

He went to his grandmother's lodge, but no one recognized in the handsome young man the one who had left them so poor and ugly. All gathered about him to listen to his wonderful story. He told them of the commands of the Sun, and a short time after made the Medicine Lodge as the Sun had commanded. This was the first Medicine Lodge.

Scarface became a great chief and all listened to his wise words. The beautiful girl came to him and said, "You are very handsome now, and a great chief, and I will marry you." But he sent her away. He married good women and lived a long time. When he died Sun Dog took him back to the Sun, where he lives forever.

Thunder Maker and Cold Maker

Thunder Maker and Cold Maker

I N ancient times, before horses had come from the south and been taught to bear burdens, the people did not move camp often, but remained in one place so long as sufficient game could be found to furnish food. They shrank from taking down their lodges and travelling over the prairie to fresh hunting-grounds, for their dogs could not pack everything, and they themselves were forced to carry heavy loads on their backs. One season they had hunted on a little stream in the foot-hills since early spring. The summer passed, the leaves began to fall, and with the approach of winter the great herds of buffalo slowly grazed out on the plains, and finally disappeared to the eastward. Hardy and warmly furred as they were they feared the deep snow and the cold of the mountain country.

The Punishment of the Stingy

When the last of the buffalo had gone, a great hunter named Low Wolf thought that it was also time for him to move. He said to the chiefs: "Come, now, the buffalo have gone; they are our food; let us too move away from the mountains and follow them."

But the chiefs said they would not break camp for a while. "Snow will not fall for one or two moons," they said, "and there are still plenty of elk, deer, moose, and other small game close by. Do not be impatient. Let us wait."

Low Wolf would not listen to them. "No," he said, "I am not a hunter of small game. The buffalo are my living, and to-morrow I shall follow them, even if I go alone."

The people thought that he was joking; but the next morning they learned that he meant what he said, for when they arose they saw that already his lodge had been taken down, and his wife and daughter were busy packing the dogs and lashing the travois on them.

"Hold on," said the chiefs, coming up; "why all this hurry? It is not safe for you to go alone. It is not right for you to take your wife and daughter out on the lonely plains.

Thunder Maker and Cold Maker

Think of all the dangers. Wait until we are ready to move."

"What the Low Wolf has said cannot be unsaid," he replied. "I told you that to-day I should start after the buffalo, and now I am going."

For several days the little family travelled eastward along the valley of the evergrowing stream, but found no buffalo. Then they turned northeast, and after four nights on the wide prairie saw before them another valley. Buffalo were all around them now, and Low Wolf said that if they could find plenty of timber and water he would be content to stay in this place until spring. There was a large river flowing through the valley, and along its banks grew groves of large cotton-woods and willows. At the edge of one of these groves the dogs were unpacked and the lodge put up where it was protected from the wind. That night, as the little family sat about the fire eating fat buffalo ribs, Low Wolf said: " Ah, how foolish were the people not to come with me; here we have a fine sheltered camp, plenty of wood, and on all sides the buffalo darken the prairie. Besides, down here it is still summer weather,

while up there where they are it is already
freezing at night."

The days passed happily. Every morning
Low Wolf went out to hunt, and his wife and
daughter dried the meat that he brought in,
tanned soft robes for sleeping and for covering,
and cut great piles of fire-wood against the cold
of approaching winter.

One evening, Plover Call, the daughter, went
out to gather the night's wood, and while she
was lashing a pile of it to carry in she happened to look up, and saw standing near a man
wearing his robe hair side out. He was facing
the river, his back towards her, but she supposed
it was her father, although it seemed strange
that he should follow her out into the timber,
as there were no signs of any enemy about.

"What are you doing there?" she asked.
"Come, I have gathered my wood; let us go
home."

The man turned towards her and lowered
his robe from his face, and she saw that he
was a stranger—a handsome young man, with
light-colored hair and a white face. Strangely
enough she was not afraid of him, for he had
a kind face, and his blue eyes looked pleasant.

Thunder Maker and Cold Maker

"Ah," he said, as he slowly drew near where she stood, "I have come from a far land. I have left my people, for something told me to go in search of a wife. When I saw you I knew that you were the one I was meant to find. Let us live together."

Plover Call forgot her wood as she looked at him. "Come with me to our lodge," she said at last, "and I will find out if it may be as you ask." When they came to it she told him to stand outside for a little.

"Father, mother," she said, as she entered the doorway, "I have found a young man out in the woods who wishes to marry me; are you willing that he should?"

"Is he strong and active?" asked Low Wolf.

"Is he well clothed and good-looking?" the mother inquired.

"Oh," said the girl, "he is everything you ask, and more; he is even strange-looking, for he has a white face, and his hair is the color of last year's prairie grass."

"Well," said Low Wolf, "it matters not about his looks, so long as he is an active man; yet it is strange that he is so different from us. Tell him to come in."

131

The Punishment of the Stingy

Plover Call went to the doorway and beckoned to the young man, and when he had entered, her father and mother motioned him to a seat, and soon began to talk to him, asking many questions. The young man replied readily to all of them, so after he had considered for a time, Low Wolf concluded to give him his daughter. The next day she and her mother began to make a new lodge, and as soon as it was finished, put up and stored with robes and clothing, food and other things, the two were married.

"I am glad that you came," the father said to the young man, "and glad to give you my good daughter. We will not be so lonely now, and if the enemy should come there will be two of us to fight them."

The fourth day after the young couple were married and had moved into the new lodge, the stranger arose early, and after a hurried meal told Plover Call that he intended to go hunting. His wife was pleased, and said that he must bring in a deer, for she wished to tan the skin and make him some moccasins.

He picked up his bow-case and quiver, slung it on his back and started, and shortly after he left the lodge, low, continuous rumbling of thunder was heard, beginning quite near the lodges, and finally dying away in the distance. Plover Call and her parents came out of their lodges, looked around, and were surprised to see that there was not a cloud in the sky; and again it was the wrong time of year for thunder. Moreover, the young man was not to be seen in any direction, although he had gone but a moment before. It was all very strange.

Evening came; the sun had gone down, and the shadow of night covered the valley, when again thunder was heard, this time far away at first, and then coming nearer. Then presently Plover Call heard something heavy fall by the doorway, and her husband entering, said: "Well, I got the deer for you. There it lies just outside."

The young woman was uneasy; she went over and consulted her father.

"Surely mysterious things are happening about here," said Low Wolf, "and I suspect your husband is not what he seems to be. Anyhow, it is well to be on the safe side; do not eat any of the deer he brought in."

The young woman went back to her lodge, cut some meat from the deer, and cooked it for

The Punishment of the Stingy

her husband. While he was eating she skinned the animal, cut it into quarters, and hung it out on a near-by bush. After the evening meal was over her father came in, and the two men talked for a long time about hunting and war, and her husband told interesting stories about his people. Listening to him, both Plover Call and her father were ashamed of their fears, and resolved to make amends by treating the young man as kindly as they knew how.

The next day the wind changed to the north, and there came a light fall of snow; no hunting was done. The following morning Plover Call's husband again started out with his bow and arrows, and, as before, as soon as he left it thundered for a long time. The fears of the little family were again aroused, and when at night the young man returned after a long rumbling of thunder, they were all frightened, and feared that something dreadful was about to happen. The hunter had brought in another deer and told how he had killed it, and where he had been hunting.

"Why," said Low Wolf, "I was out there, too, this morning; it is strange I did not see you. I should have seen your tracks anyhow."

They learned the next day that he made no tracks. When he started out they watched him; he took four steps from the lodge door, and then suddenly vanished, the thunder beginning again and rumbling away into the distance. As he disappeared, a strange-looking bird was seen flying the way the thunder was muttering. Then they knew that this person was really the thunder bird, and their hearts were filled with a great fear.

Four times the strange husband went hunting, always disappearing at the lodge door in his mysterious way, always accompanied by thunder, going and coming, never leaving any footprints beyond the lodge. Yet when at home he was just like any other young man, light-hearted, sociable, and kind to his wife. The morning after his fourth hunt he said that he must go and visit his people.

" It is a very long distance that I must travel," he said to them, " and I may be away many moons; but do not worry, for I shall return as soon as I can." With that he left the lodge, and peering through the folds of the doorway, they saw him vanish as before, and as the thunder rolled, saw the bird flying out across the valley, over the rim of the plain towards the south.

The moons came, grew, and went, but Plover Call's husband did not return. She was glad of it, and so were her parents, for they all feared his terrible, mysterious ways.

One evening the young woman was again chopping wood by the river, and, again looking up, she saw a man standing near her, wearing his robe hair side out. Again she thought it was her father, but when she addressed him he turned around, and she saw it was a stranger. At first she was sure it was her husband, but as he lowered his robe she saw that he was dark-faced and black-haired like herself. " Who are you ?" she asked. " Why are you here ?"

" I am of your race," he said, " but from a far-away tribe. I am seeking a wife; will you marry me ?"

Plover Call would not answer his question, but told him to go with her to her parents' lodge. Low Wolf decided that she might marry the stranger at once. " The other one," he said, " that Thunder Maker, has been gone a long time, and I am sure he will never return. We need another drawer of the bow in case of attack, so put up your lodge again and try to live happily."

Although he had appeared rather strangely, and, like the Thunder Maker, had said he came from a far country, there was nothing that seemed either odd or mysterious about Plover Call's new husband. He hunted with her father, prayed to Nápi, the creator, as she did, and in no respect was different from any young Blackfoot she knew. He was very kind and gentle, and the girl soon loved him with all her heart. They lived together very happily. One day, as he sat in the lodge making some arrows, the distant rumbling of thunder was heard.

"Go!" his wife cried. "Leave here at once; the man I told you of is returning."

"I will not leave this lodge," said he, calmly, "for the Thunder person, nor any one else."

"But you must," she replied; "he will be angry; and oh, I fear him. Listen! he is coming nearer. Hurry away before it is too late."

"Ah," said her husband, "you do not love me, or you would not ask this."

"It is because I do love you that I want to have you go."

"Say no more," he replied; "now that I know you love me, I shall surely stay. I do not fear him."

Suddenly the curtain of the doorway was thrown back and the Thunder Maker bounded into the lodge. He was very angry. Streams of lightning flashed continuously from his eyes. Sheets of ill-smelling smoke, mingled with blue flame, rolled in waves from his body. Plover Call shut her eyes, nearly fainting at the dreadful sight, and her heart stood still from fear.

"What are you doing here?" he cried to the man calmly scraping his arrows. "What are you doing here in my lodge? Go at once, or I will kill you where you sit."

"Do you go yourself," the other replied, "or it will be the worse for you. This is my house, and this woman whom you deserted is my wife."

Thunder Maker sprang into the air in fury, and more fearfully than ever the lightning flashed from his eyes. Raising his hand to strike, he stepped suddenly towards his enemy, but the man as quickly held up some soft, white, downy eagle feathers, and blew them from his hand, and a terrible cold, biting wind filled the lodge. Thunder Maker fell back. The

138

wind increased, and the lodge shook as if it would be blown away. Fine, sharp, stinging frost - flakes hissed in through the doorway and from under the edges of the lodge skins. Colder and colder it grew; and, trembling, quivering, his lips blue, his teeth chattering, Thunder Maker staggered to a bed and fell upon it.

" You have beaten me; your power is greater than mine," he cried. " Oh, Cold Maker, have pity!"

For Plover Call's new husband was Cold Maker, he who brings the fierce storms, the biting wind, and drifting, whirling snow from out the north. And now, as he saw his enemy gasping, shaking, and begging for mercy, as he lay on the bed, he laughed. " Will you promise never to return; never to trouble us again?" he asked. " I will go, I will go," groaned the other. " You promise? Then go, and be sure you keep your word."

The cold wind and the hazy frost ceased as suddenly as they had come. Thunder Maker staggered to his feet. He reeled out of the lodge. Lightning no longer flashed from his eyes. The blue flame and stifling smoke no longer rolled from his person. He looked very poor and sick as he disappeared.

Now that Plover Call knew who her new husband really was, she was not at all afraid of him, although he was one of the deathless ones, who, for the time, had taken the form of man. They continued to live happily together, and when summer came he went with her and her parents, and joined the great camp of the Blackfeet.

Often Cold Maker said to her people that he could not remain with them always, but he never told them when he should go away. " After I have gone," he said once, " I will try to warn you of the approach of a cold storm. When you see a raven flying about in the winter, and crying its loud notes, look out, for the cold storm will be near."

After many years Plover Call died of old age, and Cold Maker mourned. " He will leave us now," the people said. They were right. One day he disappeared and was seen no more. But his words were not forgotten. Since that time they have named the raven after him. Even to this day the raven comes to give warning of an approaching storm.

The Blindness of Pi-waṕ-ōk

The Blindness of Pi-waṕ-ōk

P I - WAṔ - ŌK, Flint - knife, was a Blood warrior; he was brave and ambitious, seldom passing a day idly in his lodge. If not away on the war-path against some distant tribe, he was sure to be out hunting. The burning heats of summer, the cold, and the piercing snow-drifting winds of winter did not keep him back, if he thought game was to be found. There were always many buffalo hides and many skins of elk, deer, and antelope stacked up about his lodge, and within were thick warm robe beds, and piles of soft buckskins, tanned by his wife Í-kai-si, the Squirrel. None knew better than the poor, the blind, and the crippled, that the parfleches piled up behind the beds, and filling the space near the doorway, contained stores of fat dried meat, rich pemmican, marrow fat, dried berries and roots, to a share of which they

143

were always welcome. The couple had no children, and they said that unless a crowd of guests feasted and smoked in their lodge of an evening, they felt lonesome. So for many years they lived, happy and prosperous, and then a great trouble came on them.

One day Pi-waṕ-ōk returned from a hunt and complained that his eyes hurt him. "They feel as if some one had thrown sand in them," he said. "When I try to see something far away, they fill with tears and everything becomes indistinct."

"Oh, that is nothing," Í-kai-si said to him, "the hard wind which you have been out in all day has made them a little sore. I'll stew some of those leaves my old grandmother used to say were good for the eyes, and after you have bathed them once or twice, no doubt you will see clearly again."

The lotion was used for a day or two, but the inflammation increased. A great doctor was called in; he looked carefully at the red lids and the thin, ever-spreading film covering the eyes, and prescribed a steam bath, into which he threw certain herbs. It did no good, and a great medicine man was sent for. He came with ceremony, dressed in a bear-skin robe, carrying a bag of mysterious medicines, and shaking his rattles as he entered the lodge. Seating himself by the patient, he asked many questions as he examined the swollen eyes. At last he inquired if Pi-wap̄-ōk had experienced unpleasant dreams of late.

"Yes," the sick man replied, "the night before this affliction came upon me, I had a terrible dream; you remember that I killed two Crow warriors this spring when we had the battle with them at the Yellow River. Well, I was fighting it all over again in my sleep. I had stabbed and taken the scalp of one Crow, and was turning to struggle with the other, when the dead one sprang up, all bleeding and sightless, the loose skin of the forehead hanging over his eyes, and with a loud cry struck me with the war-club still hanging from his wrist. Then I woke, frightened and trembling from the awful sight."

"Ah!" said the medicine man, after thinking a little. "That explains it all; the ghost of some enemy you have killed is near here, and is blinding you in some mysterious way. Well, let me get to work; perhaps I can drive him away."

The Punishment of the Stingy

He opened the medicine bag and took from it a long pipe stem painted red and black, to which was tied a small buckskin sack, ornamented with the feathers of certain small birds, and curious claws and teeth. No one but he knew what was inside the little sack; it was his secret helper. "*Hai-yu,*" he cried to it, entreatingly. "*Hai-yu,* you certain thing of the earth. Help me now; help me to drive away the ghosts from this sufferer's eyes. As you long ago told me in my dreams to do, favored one of the Sun, that I will now do. Intercede for us all here to-day; ask the Sun to have pity on us all; to grant us long life, good health, and sufficient food."

Such was his prayer. He knelt beside Pi-wap̄-ōk, and began an ancient medicine song, shaking his rattles and motioning the unseen spirit to depart. At times he picked up the long stem and blew through it on the inflamed eyes, calling out at the end of every breath: "Whooh! Ghost, retire."

"How do you feel?" he asked, when about to leave, after many songs and prayers, and blowings through the stem.

"Oh," Pi-wap̄-ōk replied, "I can't say that

146

The Blindness of Pi-wap̄-ōk

I see any plainer, but I think my eyes are not
so painful."

"Ah!" the medicine man said, "that is but
natural; you cannot recover at once; when we
have driven the ghost away for good, then it
will still take time for the eyes to become
clear."

After some days it was found that the medicine man's charms had failed. One after another, the doctors and mystery men of the tribe
were called in. This was expensive. One de-
manded two horses, another a gun and blanket,
another three horses; another would not step
inside the lodge until he had been paid ten
horses. One by one Pi-wap̄-ōk's herd changed
hands; little by little the store of soft robes
and food disappeared, and the lodge became
bare. But the afflicted one did not get well.
For a time he could see objects dimly, then
they became mere shadows; then the light went
out entirely. Pi-wap̄-ōk was blind.

It was hard for the man who had led such
an active life to sit idly in his lodge day after
day. He visited but little from lodge to lodge,
for he did not like to ask any one to lead him
about here and there. His wife was kind,

cheering him with her constant talk and making light of their great misfortune. She worked hard to provide things as of old, by tanning for a share the hides and skins brought in by hunters. The people were all kind. They did not forget how generous the blind one had been in his prosperous days, and they came daily to relieve his poverty with gifts of meat, and even tongues and pemmican. Of an evening the chiefs and warriors would assemble in his lodge as before, to smoke and talk and cheer his spirits. Through all the pain, and the darkness of constant night, Pi-waṗ-ok kept up a good heart, though at times, when he thought of the sunlight shimmering over the yellow prairie and painting the tops of the distant mountains with wondrous color, he was very sad to think that he was never again to behold it all, never again to join in the chase, never again to experience the fierce joy of battle. One thing that kept him up was the thought that by some good chance he might, some day, be cured. He remembered the stories of the ancient ones who had been made well by their brothers, the animals of the plain and forest, of the air and the water, and he thought that they might help

148

The Blindness of Pi-wap̄-ōk

him too, if only he had an opportunity to meet them.

The people were camping along the foothills of the mountains, and one evening, after a long day's travel, the lodges were pitched by a wooded stream, and right under a high sandstone cliff which formed one side of the valley. The next morning, while yet the people slept and even the dogs were quiet, while not a stir of any kind broke the stillness of the camp, Pi-wap̄-ōk, restlessly turning on his bed, heard the shrill cry of a bald eagle (Ksik-i-kinni, white-head), now near, now far, as it circled around and around above the valley. In his mind he saw the great bird soar, now high, now low, with scarcely a movement of its powerful wings, saw the flash of golden light on its body as it turned to the rising sun. "Ah," he thought, "if my sight were only as good as that bird's, how happy I should be! Far up in the air, it looks down upon the world, and nothing escapes its eye, from the great brown buffalo quietly grazing to the little ground squirrel hunting about its hole for a root of grass."

Presently the camp awoke to another day of

The Punishment of the Stingy

the chase, of toil, of feasting, and of play.
Í-kai-si arose, built a fire, and cooked the morning meal. A friend dropped in to share it and
tell of a recent exciting bear hunt. Pi-waṕ-ōk
scarcely heard him, for he was still thinking of
the great bird swinging so strong and free in
the blue sky above. All at once he realized that
here, perhaps, was the opportunity he had long
sought; here, close by, was a "little brother,"
as his fathers called them, more keen-eyed than
any other living thing. Surely it knew how
to keep the eyes bright and clear, how to cure
them if they became diseased. "Friend," he
said to his guest, "this morning, when all was
still, I heard a whitehead sounding its cry as
it circled around above us. Did you happen to
see it?"

"Yes," the man replied, "it has a nest here,
and just as I came in I saw it carrying
something to feed its young. Far up on the
cliff by which we are camped is a short pine-
tree, growing out from the climbing rock;
there, in the branches, the bird has built its
home."

"Friend," Pi-waṕ-ōk cried; "it is as I
thought: my chance has come. I beg you to

150

guide me to that place, for I believe the traveller of the sky can cure me."

"*Hai-ya,*" the friend exclaimed, "you know not what you ask. With my good eyes, and seeing plainly where to cling and step, it would be a hard task to reach that height; for you it would be sure death to attempt the climb."

"Even so," the blind one replied, "yet must I try to do it. Death comes in many ways. It stares us in the face at every turn. Wherever we go, whatever we do, it lies in wait for us, like a panther for the deer by a forest trail. I am not afraid; have pity and help me try to reach that nest."

Í-kai-si cried, and begged him to think no more of such a dangerous thing; the friend told how straight and high the cliff was, how difficult to climb, but they talked in vain. He said that if no one would help him, he would go alone, on until he fell and died. At length, seeing that he was not to be turned from this which he had set his mind upon, the friend consented to be his guide, and they started.

It was but a few steps to the foot of the cliff, where the fallen rocks made a sloping hill; they soon surmounted this, and then the climb began. Sometimes they were side by side, the leader guiding the blind one's hands and feet, and again he was ahead, and reaching down would pull Pi-waṕ-ōk up on a narrow shelf. All the people of the camp stood watching them with wide-staring eyes, and as the two went on, higher and higher, over places where it seemed there was no jutting rock to offer foothold, they held their breath, fearing, expecting, that the next step would be the climbers' last.

Pi-waṕ-ōk's courage won. At last, tired and breathless, they came to where the gnarled and stunted tree hung to the cliff's face by its giant roots. "*Hai!*" said the guide; "I never thought we would reach it; here we are at last. And now, what next?"

"Help me up into the nest."

"That I cannot do. There is no room for more than one. The limb would break if both of us were on it."

"Then," said Pi-waṕ-ōk, "I will go alone," and he began to climb out on the trunk, his friend telling him just where to reach for a hold on the spreading branches. Then came the most dangerous feat of all, to climb over the rim of the wide and loose-sticked nest; but that too was accomplished, and the tired man lay down in its hollow beside the scared and hissing fledglings. "Go," he called out to his friend, "go and leave me for a time here alone."

The young man climbed on up to the summit of the cliff, and walked away to a distant point, where he waited until he should be called.

Pi-waṕ-ōk lay motionless; the young birds ceased their frightened cries, and all was still save for the breeze, which sung through the tree-top with a mournful sound. If the limb on which the nest was built gave way from his added weight, he knew that he would fall upon the rocks far below, a crushed and shapeless mass. It was an uneasy and frightful thought.

And now from afar the parent bird espied him in the nest, and swooped down with a terrible rushing roar, like far-off thunder. Down, down, she came, swift as an arrow, to the very edge of the nest, and then soared upward with a bound, the rushing air behind swaying the tree as if a hurricane was passing. Again and again, four times in all, the bird made a rushing dive at the helpless man, and each time he heard its nearing cry he prayed, crying out that he had not come to harm its young, but to ask its aid. And at last the whitehead seemed to understand, for after the fourth fierce rush, it slowly sailed around and settled on the edge of the nest.

"*Hai-yu,*" Pi-waṕ-ōk cried, "be you male or female, father or mother of these young birds, as you love them, pity me."

"I am their mother," the bird replied, "and, since you have called upon me in their name, say what is in your mind; I will help you if I can."

Then the blind one told of his affliction, and how through great danger and sore distress of mind he had climbed the cliff, hoping the great bird might cure him.

"Alas," said the whitehead when he had finished, "what you ask is beyond my power; nor could my husband, who is away hunting, help you. None of my kind could make you see again, for we have never had occasion to treat the eyes. We live to great age, but our eyes remain strong and clear to the very end."

Pi-waṕ-ōk wept. "Alas!" he cried, "how

154

my hopes have fallen. This long and dangerous climb, after all, brings no relief."

"Not so," said the bird. "I cannot give you sight, but in other ways I can do much for you. Here is a feather from my tail; take it, and keep it carefully, and you shall live to old age. And since you are helpless in your blindness, I will do more. I will teach you many wonderful things, and will give you power to heal the sick. Then you will not sit sad and idle in your lodge. The people will keep coming for you to go here and there to heal them and to practise your mysterious rites, and you will be so busy that you will forget your blindness."

Then the bird began, and through the long morning taught Pi-waṕ-ōk, showing him the secret of many wonderful things, telling him how and what to use for certain ailments. It took a long time to explain it all, and just as the bird finished, the blind one fell asleep.

After a little he awoke. "Put out your hand and feel," the whitehead said. He did so and found he was lying on grassy ground.

"You are on the prairie at the top of the cliff," the bird continued; "your friend is sitting away over there on a point. Rise up and motion him to come, for I must leave you now."

When the young man saw him beckoning, he came running with all his might. "Ah!" he cried, as he came near, "you are cured."

"No," Pi-waṕ-ōk replied. "I am still as blind as ever."

"Then how came you here? How could you climb that awful cliff and still be blind?"

"I do not know," said Pi-waṕ-ōk. "I was asleep in the whitehead's nest, and when I awoke I was here."

The way home was easy, for they followed the rim of the valley to a point beyond the cliff, and then descended a sloping hill. And when they had arrived at camp the people came crowding around to hear all that had happened.

As the whitehead had said, Pi-waṕ-ōk became a great medicine man and healer of the sick, and, through the secret power that the bird gave him, he was able to do many strange things. He and his wife, Í-kai-si, lived to a great age. He was the greatest healer the Bloods have ever had.

Ragged Head

Ragged Head

ANY years ago there was a Nez Percé Indian whose name was Ragged Head. He wore the long hair on the front of his head tied up in a bunch, and the ends hanging over were ragged and of different lengths. This was why they gave him this name. This man was a great warrior. He could not be killed. When he was a young man his dream helper had come to him in his sleep and had spoken to him, saying:

"My son, you are a man who need not fear to go into battle, for neither arrow nor bullet nor lance nor knife can hurt you. You may rush into the very midst of the enemy, and they will all run away from you. Take courage, therefore, take great courage." Then his dream helper smoked with him.

But when the dream helper had spoken to

him in his sleep, and had told him that he need not be afraid of his enemies, and had smoked with him, it had said further:

" My son, some day you must die, and it may be that you will be killed by your enemy, for there is one thing that can hurt you. Only one thing, but of this you must be careful. If you should be shot with a ramrod, it will pierce your flesh and you will die."

After Ragged Head had returned to the camp, he told this part of his dream to no one, except to two of his close friends, for he did not wish it to be known and talked about. None of these three men thought much about it, nor felt afraid, for every one knows that people when they are in battle and are trying to kill their enemies, do not shoot ramrods at them, but bullets.

When this man went to war he did not carry a gun, nor arrows, nor a lance. His weapon was a great war-club, made from the butt of an elk antler. With this he used to beat down his enemies. In the end of the club he had put a lash, and he used it also as a riding quirt.

Every summer Ragged Head used to cross the mountains from his country to the plains, to hunt buffalo and to make war on the Piegans. When he saw a party of his enemies, he would charge down upon them, shaking his war-club and shouting out the war-cry; and when the Piegans saw who it was that was coming they all tried to get out of his way, for they knew that he could not be killed, and that they could not do anything to hurt him. So he killed many of his enemies, and had great fame among his own people and among those against whom he fought. He was a leader of war-parties and always successful. Everybody was afraid of him, for all people knew that he had strong spiritual power, and that he could not be killed.

It was early summer. The grass had started. The snow was melting on the mountains. Already the streams were high. It was time to go to war.

From their camp on the plains a party of Piegans set out on the war-path to cross the mountains and take horses from their enemies on the other side—Snakes, Flat Heads, or Nez Percés. On foot they made their way along the lower hills, climbed up through the narrow pass, and at length stood on the top of the mountain range, from which they could look out over the lower country to the west. There, in the wide gray plain before them, they could trace the winding courses of many streams, and from some of them rose smokes which showed that people were camped there, and they knew that these people were their enemies.

While they were stopping here, overlooking the country, the leader of the war-party said to his young men:

" Now, here we will separate and go off in small parties to see what we can discover, and after ten nights we will all meet again at the Round Butte at the foot of this mountain, and return to our camp together."

So here the party divided, going off by twos and threes to try to find the camps of their enemies.

There were two young Piegans who went off together. The younger of the two carried a bow and arrows, and the other had an old shot-gun the barrels of which had been cut off short, so that he could carry it under his robe without its being seen. The tube which had held the ramrod in its place had been broken off, and there was no way to carry the rod except in

162

the barrel of the gun. When the boy was shooting, he held the ramrod in his hand.

After a few days' travel these young men
found a trail where people had passed not long
before, and following this trail, they saw a
camp, and hid themselves near by to wait for
night and then to go to it and take horses. This
was the camp of the Nez Percés, and Ragged
Head was its chief.

In the night, after it was dark and the camp
had become quiet, the young men crept down
to the river, close to the lodges, to see what they
might do. The older boy said to his companion,
" I will go first into the camp and see how things
are there, and perhaps take a horse or two, and
then I will come back here and tell you, and
we can both go back and take more horses if
all goes well." The other said, " It is good;
I will wait for you here."

The older boy crossed the stream and crept
into the camp and looked about. The people
were sleeping; it was all quiet, and in front
of the lodges were tied many fine horses. He
found two that he liked, and cut the ropes that
held them, and led them back across the stream
to where he had left his friend; but when he

reached the place his friend was not waiting there. So the young man led the horses into the brush and tied them, and crossed the stream again for more. As he was wading through the water, carrying his gun muzzle up so that the ramrod should not fall out, and when he was near the other bank, he saw a man standing there, and thought it was his friend.

When he came close to him he said: " Why did you not wait for me on the other side, as you said you would ?" The person did not answer, but stretched out his left hand and caught the boy by the hair, pulled him forward, and raised a great club, as if to strike him.

Then the young Piegan was frightened. He put up his left hand to ward off the blow, and with his right he pushed the muzzle of his shot-gun against the person's body and pulled both triggers. The gun went off. The man fell, and the young Piegan quickly ran away.

At the sound of the shot all the Nez Percés rushed out of their lodges and up and down the stream to learn what had happened. On the river-bank they found Ragged Head dead. In his body was the splintered ramrod.

Nothing Child

Nothing Child

LONG time ago there lived in the
Blackfoot camp a young man who
did not like company. He preferred
to be alone. He had a wife but no
children, and one young brother who lived with
him. This was his only close relation. This
man had a tame bear, which he had caught when
it was a little cub. During the day he went
hunting, and set traps and snares for game,
and at night, when he returned to the camp,
he did not go about visiting at the other lodges,
but stayed at home by himself.

One day he thought he would move away
from the village and camp alone—just his own
lodge. They started, the man and his wife,
and the young brother and the bear. They
went up towards the mountains, and camped in
the timber. The man hunted and killed plenty
of game, and they stayed there for a long time.

The Punishment of the Stingy

While the older brother was hunting, the younger one used to stay at home, making arrows and shooting with them, and at length he became a very good shot.

After a time the younger brother had grown big, and he was a handsome boy, and the woman fell in love with him, but he took no notice of her.

One day, while the young brother was sitting in the lodge making arrows, and the woman was outside tanning a hide, she called to him and said, " Oh, brother, come out and kill this pretty bird that is here," but the boy was busy smoothing his arrows, and paid no attention. Pretty soon she asked him again, and then a third time, and when she called him the fourth time he got up and went outside and killed the bird and gave it to her, and then went into the lodge again and kept on working at his arrows. He did not stop and talk with her. Pretty soon the boy went off into the timber to try his arrows. The bear was lying by the door of the lodge.

The woman was angry at the boy because he took no notice of her, and she made up her mind that she would be revenged on him. So

Nothing Child

while he was gone she scratched and bruised her face and tore her hair.

At night her husband came home, and when he looked at his wife he saw that her face was scratched and swollen and her hair all pulled about. He sent out his young brother to hang up the meat that he had brought in, and the boy went leaving arrows lying by the fire to dry. While he was gone the woman said to her husband, " Your brother has beaten me because I asked him to shoot a pretty bird for me." She showed her husband the scratches and bruises she had made on herself, and said, " See how he has used me."

When the man heard this he was angry, but he said nothing. When the boy came back from hanging up the meat, he looked for his arrows but did not see them. Then he asked, " Where have you put my arrows ?" but no one answered, and at length he saw the ends of them among the ashes, for his brother had thrown them into the fire. When the boy saw that his arrows had been burned he cried, and taking his robe and his bow and what arrows he had left, he went out of the lodge. He made up his mind that he could not live here with his brother

The Punishment of the Stingy

any longer, and decided to go away. The bear, which all this time had been lying by the door of the lodge, listening, was angry at the lies the woman had told, and at what her husband had done, and he got up and went out and followed the boy. They travelled for a while and then slept, and the next day went on again, going towards the mountains.

For two days they travelled, and on the third day, as they were going along, the boy saw sitting in a tree-top a bird that was white as snow, and different from any bird that he had seen before. He took an arrow from his quiver and shot the bird, and as it fell, it caught among the branches and lodged there. He threw sticks at it, but could not knock it down, so he made up his mind that he would climb the tree and get the bird and his arrow. When he had tightened his belt and was just about to climb the tree, the bear spoke to him and said: " You had better not do this. If you go up there something bad may happen. It will be better to let the things go." But the boy was very anxious to get that bird and his arrow, and would not listen to the bear's words, but began to climb the tree.

Nothing Child

He reached the branch where the arrow was, but when he stretched out his hand to take it it moved up a little higher, just beyond his fingers. So he climbed higher and again reached for the arrow, and again it moved up a little higher. He kept climbing and climbing, with the arrow always moving in front of him, until at last he climbed out of sight.

For the rest of the day the bear stood at the foot of the tree, looking upward and whining and moaning for his friend, but he saw nothing of him. About sundown all the boy's clothing came tumbling down together, but nothing was seen of the boy. The bear would not leave the tree. He waited there, hoping to see what had become of the boy, but that was the last of him. He saw him no more.

After the boy and the bear had left the camp, the older brother kept thinking of what had taken place. When they did not come back he felt lonesome and sad, and began to fear that something would happen to his young brother, and at last he made up his mind that he would start out and learn what had become of him. He left his lodge and set out in the direction the two had taken. He found their

171

trail and followed it, and after two days came to the tree and there saw the bear, standing on his hind feet and resting his paws against the tree. The man asked the bear what had become of the boy, but the bear would not reply to him. He asked him the same question again, and a third and a fourth time, and then the bear answered and said: " All this trouble has come upon us through your fault, because you listened to the lies your woman told you. Your brother has climbed this tree and has gone out of sight, and now for three days I have stood here, waiting for him to come down. His clothing has fallen down from up above, but he does not return." They waited by the tree longer, but the boy did not come down, and at length the man said to the bear: " My brother is gone. He will never come back. We had better go back to the camp where we can live." The bear went back with him.

On their way the bear told the man how it really had been, and that it was not the boy who had hurt the woman, but that she had done it herself, and in this way had caused his brother to lose his life. Then the man was angry, and when they came near to the lodge he took an arrow from his quiver and shot his wife, and her shadow went to the sand-hills.

That night the man said to the bear, " Well, we are only two now, and for myself, I have decided to stay here and starve to death, and as for you, you had better leave me and go your way and make your living as all bears do." So the bear went away and did not return.

One night while the man was lying asleep, he dreamed of the bear; and the bear spoke to him and said: " My brother, listen to the words that I speak to you, and do now what I tell you to. Go back to the old camp of your people, to the cliff where they drive the buffalo, the piś kun, and wait there. A camp of your people is moving towards that place. They are very poor and have but little to eat. It may be that you can help them. Be sure to do exactly as I tell you from this time on, and in the days to come you will be unhappy no longer, but will have plenty of everything and will have full life. Now I wish you to-morrow, when you awake, to eat up your lodge and everything that is in it. This seems to you like a hard thing, something that cannot be done, but, by the power that I give you, you will be able to do it."

When the man awoke, in the morning, he thought for a long time over what the bear had said to him in his sleep, and how it had said that in the time to come he would be poor no longer, but would have full life, and how it had said that it would give him that power, and he made up his mind to do as the bear had told him. He tore down his lodge and began to eat it, and found that this was not a hard thing to do. He ate the lodge and the lining, his clothing, his wife's things— everything that he could find in the lodge, and then took his bow and arrows and started to go to the cliff as the bear had told him to.

Now since the bear had left, the man had had no food to eat, and on his journey he found himself getting weak and growing smaller. When he reached the cliff there was no camp there, so he waited, and all the time he kept getting weaker, and smaller and smaller, until he was no bigger than a year-old child. He thought now that he would surely die, and hid himself under a bunch of rye grass.

The next day the people moved in and camp-

Nothing Child

ed at this place. An old woman went out to
get some grass for her bed, and while she was
gathering it, she heard a sound as if a little
child were crying. She went in the direction
of the sound, and under a bunch of rye grass
she found a little child. She carried him into
the camp and took good care of him. When
the chief of the camp heard of how she had
found the child, he said to the old woman,
" Take good care of that child; he was put there
for some good purpose."

As time passed the child grew fatter and
stronger, and the old woman grew fond and
proud of him. They called him Kiś tap i
pokau (Nothing Child.)

Near this camp stood a tree, and every day
an eagle came and alighted in the tree. The
chief had tried many times to kill this eagle,
and so had other men, but no one could kill it.
When they found that no one could kill it, they
wanted it all the more. The chief had two
very pretty daughters, and at length he said
that he would give his daughters to any one
who would kill this eagle. When this was called out through the camp by the old crier, all
the young men came out to try to kill the eagle,

175

but no one could do it. At last Nothing Child
said to the old woman, " Grandmother, make
me some arrows so that I can kill the eagle."
The old woman laughed when he asked her this,
but she was very fond of him, so she tied a
string to a deer's rib for a bow and made him
some little arrows, and he set out to kill the
eagle. When the young men who had been
shooting at the eagle saw the child coming with
the tiny bow, they laughed and made fun of
him, but Nothing Child fitted a little arrow
on the string of his bow, and shot and killed
the eagle. Then all who were standing by were
astonished, but they said, " It must have been
a chance shot." The eagle was taken to the
chief's lodge, and they told him it had been
killed by the Nothing Child. So he told his
daughters to go and marry the found boy.

But the young men were not satisfied with
this decision. They said that it was not fair,
that the boy had made a chance shot, and they
asked the chief to try their skill in some other
way. So the chief told the young men that they
might again try their luck for the young girls,
and that whoever killed a white wolf with a
black tail should have his daughters. All the

men went out from the camp and built their
wooden traps, and Nothing Child also went
out and made a wooden trap. The next morning they all went out to visit their traps, and
in almost all the traps they found something—
wolves, foxes, badgers, and other animals. Some
of the wolves were white all over, and some
were white with gray tails, but no one had
a white wolf with a black tail. The Nothing
Child, with his grandmother, went out from the
camp to his trap in a different direction from
the rest, and in their trap they found a
white wolf with a black tail. They took it
into camp and to the chief's lodge, and when he
saw it he said that this was the wolf he wanted.

Now all the young men in the camp were
jealous of the Nothing Child, for it was certain
that he would get the chief's daughters for his
wives. So they went to the chief and asked
him to try his people once more, that they
thought that the Nothing Child had not killed
the wolf fairly. So the chief now said: " Whoever will bring me a white fox with a black-
tipped tail shall have my daughters. This will
be the last trial, and after this no one need
complain."

M   177

The Punishment of the Stingy

The young men set their traps all over the prairie, but Nothing Child asked his grandmother to go with him, and he went to a place far from all the others and there set his trap. The next morning the young men all went out to look at their traps. Some had foxes and some had other animals, but when Nothing Child went to his trap, he found in it a white fox with a black-tipped tail, and when it was taken to the chief's lodge he said that this was the fox he meant, and he told his daughters to get ready and go and marry the Nothing Child. The youngest girl was willing to do what her father ordered, but the elder was not.

They put on their finest clothing and left their father's lodge and started for Nothing Child's home. As they walked along, the elder girl said to her sister, " I am not going to marry this child, to be laughed at by everybody." The younger sister said, " I am going to do what my father told me to. It is better to do so. Besides that, the Nothing Child must be a very powerful person. See how many wonderful things he has done." The elder girl said, " Well, I am not going to his lodge. I am going to marry Masto pau (Raven Arrow)." This

Nothing Child

was a young man who had the power to turn himself into a raven whenever he wished. So the elder girl went her way to Raven Arrow, but the younger kept on towards Nothing Child's lodge.

When the girl came to the lodge and went in, the old woman told her to sit down. Nothing Child was playing at the back of the lodge. The girl said, " My father sent me to sit beside the person who killed the eagle, the white wolf with the black tail, and the white fox with the black-tipped tail." Nothing Child said, " I am the person who did that, but I do not want any woman to sit beside me." The girl answered: " My father sent me to sit beside you, and I shall stay here. I am not going home any more." When the boy saw that the girl was resolved to stay, he said, " Very well, you shall be my wife." So she stayed, and was pleasant and nice with the boy and played with him, and he liked her. She saw that he was very poor, but she seemed to take no notice of that.

At this time the camp was very short of food. The young men scouted far and near over the prairie, but could find no buffalo. It was· a hard time; everybody was hungry. One day Nothing Child said to his wife: "Now you stay here for a while. I am going away for a time. I am going to try to find a band of buffalo and bring them into camp." He made ready for his journey and started. After he had travelled a long way he came to a wet, marshy place near the mountains, where in summer many buffalo had been. Here he gathered up buffalo chips, and made great piles of them in a row, and when he had finished, he went back some way, and then came running and shouting towards the piles of chips. When he got close to them he stopped, and then went back again, and again came running and shouting upon the chips, but nothing happened. He repeated this a third and a fourth time, and the fourth time, when he got near the piles, the chips turned into buffaloes and rushed off over the prairie, and Nothing Child ran them towards the camp and drove them over the cliff into the piś kun, so that once more the camp was supplied with meat.

The next day Nothing Child told his wife to go to her father's lodge for the day, and not to return until night. After the girl had gone he spoke to his grandmother and said: " Grandmother, you have seen what strange things I have done, and you can see that I have some power. That power which I have was given to me by a bear that has helped me, and because I have done just what he told me to I have been able to accomplish the things that you have seen me do. I do not know the secret of my power, but I know that I have it. Now, Grandmother, I want you to do something for me. I want you to take a rope and tie me by the feet to the lodge poles, so that I may hang head downward from the poles. I am little, and you can easily hold me up." The old woman did as he had told her, and he hung there head downward. Pretty soon he opened his mouth, and a little piece of cowskin stuck out. Nothing Child took hold of this and began to pull on it, and more and more came out, and at last he had pulled out the whole of his old lodge, and then he pulled out the lining, and afterwards many of his old belongings. When he had eaten all these things they had been old, but now they were new and white, and finely ornamented. The lodge was painted, the woman's clothing was beautifully work-

The Punishment of the Stingy

ed with porcupine quills; there was a new full set of war clothing for himself—all very fine.

After he had done this Nothing Child asked the old woman to untie him, and when he was on his feet again it was seen that he was no longer a child, but a full-grown man, very handsome. He told the old woman to set up the new lodge, and she did so. When his wife returned she was surprised to see all the new things. They looked strange to her. Also her husband, who, when she last saw him, was a small boy and rather ugly, was now a big, fine-looking man. The girl was pleased with the change, and now they lived together for a long time very happily.

After a time Raven Arrow became jealous of Nothing Child because of his power, but Nothing Child did not notice this, and, because Raven Arrow was poor, he asked him to come and live with him in his lodge. He did so, and they lived together for some time, and now the elder daughter of the chief was sorry that she had not done as her father had told her to.

One day, in the early summer, Nothing Child's wife said to him, "Oh, how much I would like some fresh berries to eat!" He said to her: "Do you want some fresh berries? Well, now, go out and gather a lot of sarvis berry branches and bring them to me here in the lodge." The woman did as he had told her, and brought in the bushes and threw them down on the floor of the lodge. Then Nothing Child took a tanned elk-skin and covered the bushes with it. In a short time he told his wife to take the skin off the brush, and when she did so she was astonished, for she found the twigs loaded with fine ripe berries, as though they were growing.

Now, when Raven Arrow's wife saw this she felt that she too would like some berries, and she asked her husband if he could do this. But he said: "No. It is useless for me to try to do things that I know I cannot do. I can change myself into a raven and can do many other things, but I cannot make ripe berries grow in the spring, nor can I do many other things that Nothing Child does."

After some time it happened that food again became scarce in the camp, and the chief sent word to his son-in-law, asking him if he could not again bring the buffalo into the camp, as he had done before. The hunters had been out and had travelled far over the prairie, but they could see nothing. Nothing Child sent word back that this was a hard thing he was asked to do; he feared he could not do it, but he would try.

He made ready for his journey and started, travelling a long way looking for the buffalo, but he found none. He then went to the marsh where he had made buffalo before, and again made many little piles of buffalo chips in rows, and again went back some distance and then came charging down on the piles running and shouting. And the fourth time he did this the piles of chips changed into real buffalo and started running. And Nothing Child ran the herd over the cliff, as he had done before, and again the camp was supplied with meat. In this herd was one white buffalo. His wife met him at the cliff, and he told her that this white buffalo was hers. That she must be careful of the skin when she had taken it off.

His wife told her husband that Raven Arrow had changed himself into a raven, and had flown away to look for buffalo, saying that if he found any he was going to drive them out of the country. This made Nothing Child

Nothing Child

angry, but he said nothing and waited. One day, as he was sitting by the fire, Raven Arrow, in the shape of a white raven, flew into the lodge and lit on the ground by him. When Nothing Child saw him he seized him and tied him by the feet to a lodge pole high up in the smoke and kept him there until he was nearly dead from the smoke. At last Nothing Child asked him if he would promise never again to drive the buffalo away from the people. Raven Arrow promised that he would never again do so, and Nothing Child untied him and let him down, when he changed into a man again. Up to that time ravens had always been white, but ever since the smoking that this raven got they have been black.

Nothing Child and his wife lived to full age and always had plenty of everything.

Shield Quiver's Wife

Shield Quiver's Wife

T HERE were two young men growing up in the Blackfoot camp. They
were both good warriors and were
making great names for themselves.
One was lucky in taking horses. His name was
Shield Quiver. The other was fortunate in
killing enemies when he went to war. He was
called Bearhead. When either of the two went
to war, he always had a big party to follow him.
Bearhead was jealous of Shield Quiver, because
he always brought in horses.

One time the Blackfeet were camped at the
Bear Paw Mountains, when Shield Quiver
made up his mind that he would go off on the
war-path. When he said that he was going,
a large party intended to go with him.

Before he started the chief of the camp sent
for him to come to his lodge, saying that he
wished to speak with him. When Shield Quiver

had come to the lodge the chief said: "Here, my young man, now that you are going to war, take my daughter with you, for you are the man that ought to have her. But you will have to be on your guard against Bearhead. He wants my daughter, and for a long time has been trying to get her, but I cannot let him have her. He has a bad disposition. He has had many wives, but, after living with them for a short time, he has got angry with them and killed them. I am afraid that if I give him my daughter he might kill her."

Shield Quiver thought for a little while, and then said: "Very well; I will go to war, and I will take your daughter with me, but if I go with a woman I cannot let men go with me. I shall have to go alone."

The chief said: "I cannot say anything about that. You will do what you think best. I cannot advise you."

So Shield Quiver took the chief's daughter for his wife. He said to his followers: "Now I am going to war, but you men cannot come with me. I shall be gone two moons, and then I will come back. I am going alone."

He started with his young wife, and they

went towards the Snake Country. They travelled for a good many days, until they came to a range of mountains and crossed it. Then they went on towards the head waters of a stream that they could see a long way off. When they reached this stream they found that the Snakes had been camped there, and had moved away that day. The fires were still burning in the camp.

When Shield Quiver found that the Snakes had only just moved from there, he said to his wife: " Here, let us get back in the brush. These people are not far from here. They may see us. We must hide ourselves." They went back into the brush and hid.

While they were waiting in the brush a dark cloud came up in the west, and it looked as if they were going to have a storm. Shield Quiver said to his wife: " While we have to wait, I will fix up a little shelter of brush here, so that we may keep dry; but to-night we will go to the camp and take horses."

" Very well," said his wife, " while you are fixing the place, I will go around the point and into the old camp and will see if I can find anything there that has been left behind."

The Punishment of the Stingy

For often something may be forgotten and left in the camp.

That day the Snakes had left this camp, and had moved over to another creek. The head chief of the Snakes had but one son, a fine-looking young man—the handsomest in all the Snake camp. That morning, before they moved, he had painted himself and had dressed himself finely, and after he had finished he handed his mother his sack of paints to pack. While his mother was packing, she put down the paints in a little patch of brush, near the lodge, and then went away and forgot them.

When the young man came into camp that evening he said to his mother, "Mother, where are my paints?" Then his mother remembered that she had left them in the camp they had just come from. She said, "Oh, my son, I forgot the sack, and left it in a little patch of brush just back of where the lodge stood." The young man caught up a horse and went back to get it that same evening.

When he rode into the old camp, and came to where the lodge had been, he saw there on her knees a woman with an elk robe over her head, and in her hands his paints, which she was looking at. When he rode up to her, and when she looked up at him, he saw that she was very pretty, and he liked her as soon as he looked at her; and she, when she saw him, so handsome and finely dressed and painted, liked him.

He made signs to her, saying, " Who are you, and what tribe do you belong to?" She signed back to him that she was a Blackfoot. Then she asked him, " Who and what are you?" He answered, " A Snake." He asked her by signs, " Where is the party that you are with?" She said, " There are only two of us." He said, " Come, get on my horse behind me here, and let us go to my camp." She answered: " No, there are some things that I have here that I want to get. Then I will go with you." Then she thought a little and said: " The only other person here is my husband. Why do you not kill him? I will help you." The Snake said: " It is good. I will do it." The girl said to him: " I will go to him, and do you creep through the brush, and as soon as I see you I will throw my robe around him and hold him, and you can kill him with your lance."

The Punishment of the Stingy

She went back to the camping-place, and when she got there her husband was stooping down hobbling the horses. The Snake was right behind her, creeping through the brush. She walked up to her husband and threw herself down over him, and kissed him while he was hobbling the horses. He looked up at her and laughed. He thought she was only playing with him. In a minute he heard the footsteps of some one coming, running, and he said, "Look out! here comes somebody," and he tried to throw her off, but he could not. He raised himself up while she clung to him, and the Snake made a pass at him with the lance, but he was afraid of killing the woman, and he missed the man, and Shield Quiver caught hold of the lance. He kept calling to his wife: "Let go of me. This man is trying to kill me. He will kill us both. Let us try to save ourselves."

Shield Quiver and the Snake wrestled and tugged backward and forward to see who should get the lance. They were both strong men, and at length the shaft broke, and Shield Quiver held the piece on which was the head. Then he jumped back and shook off his wife, and

194

Shield Quiver's Wife

rushed at the Snake and thrust the lance into his breast, and so killed him with his own lance.

Then he turned to his wife and said: "Now, woman, I have killed this man that you have tried to help, and I would like to have you tell me what is the reason that you acted as you did, and tried to help him to kill me."

Then the woman explained her reasons, and said: "When I left you I went into the camp and found this sack of paint, and while I was looking at it he came up and asked me to go to his camp with him, and I liked him, and thought that I would go with him. So we laid a plan to kill you before we went to camp."

Shield Quiver said to her: "Now, woman, listen. Bearhead wanted you. He has had a good many women, and he has killed all that he had. Through pity I took you. I never expected to take a wife. I will not do anything to you for what you have done to me, but will take good care of you and will give you back to your father."

He scalped the Snake and took everything that he had. The woman was crying hard. He asked her what she was crying about, and she

195

The Punishment of the Stingy

answered: "I am crying for my lover, who is dead." He said: "Saddle up your horse. We will go home."

They started, and after many days' travel reached the Blackfoot camp. It was in the night. The next morning Shield Quiver said to his wife: "Put on your best clothing. I told you I was going to give you back to your father, and I am going to take you there this morning. So get ready to go."

The woman put on her best clothes, and painted herself up nicely, and they started off to the old chief's lodge. The old chief was glad to see his son-in-law and his daughter back again. No one knew that Shield Quiver had killed a Snake. He had not spoken of it to any one. After they had sat down the young man reached down into his belt and drew out the scalp and said: "Here, old man, here is all I have done on this journey. I have taken no horses, but I have killed a Snake. I have killed your daughter's lover. It is only by the help and the power of the Sun that you see me here to-day. Your daughter tried to kill me on this trip, while I was fighting with this Snake Indian. I am afraid to live with her,

196

and have brought her back to you again. This is the best I can do, to give you this scalp and your daughter back again." When Shield Quiver had said this he got up and walked out of the lodge, and went back to his own home. The old man said nothing.

The girl had two brothers, and both were sitting in the lodge while Shield Quiver was speaking; and when they had heard the story told, and had thought about it, they got up, and each took hold of one of the girl's arms, and they led her out of the lodge. Then they said to her: " You cannot live here with us. You had better go and join your dead Snake lover."

So they killed her there.

The Beaver Stick

The Beaver Stick

IN ancient times, long before the people had found horses and used them instead of dogs to bear burdens and drag lodge poles, there lived Manyan—New Robe—an orphan.

New Robe's parents had died when he was a little child, and he was brought up by an old woman who also died before he grew up to be a man. His parents, hopeful for his future, had given their son a good name, but in all his life up to the time he was seventeen or eighteen years old, he had never worn a new robe or any other new article of clothing. The cast-off garments of the well-to-do were thought good enough for him. He was always dirty and ragged, and his matted and tangled hair hung low over his forehead, and almost hid his sore red eyes. Somewhere he had picked up an old bow, but it had no strength; and even if it had been

201

strong and full of quick spring, the broken-pointed flint heads of his arrows would not have pierced the flesh of any large animal. He had an old flint knife, but its edge was so ragged and blunted that it would scarcely cut a piece of boiled meat.

Yet New Robe lived along contentedly enough, for he knew nothing better than all this. He never thought that he was different from other young men, until one day he chanced to overhear the conversation of some young women. He was lying half asleep in a patch of willows when the girls came along, and, stopping near him, sat down and kept on talking.

"Well," said one, "you have each told your choice, but you have not spoken of the very handsomest and nicest of all the young men. Why have you forgotten New Robe?"

They all shrieked with laughter—she who had spoken most of all—and then began to jest about him, and New Robe's face grew hot as he heard the many unkind things they said about his appearance and his poverty. One of the girls, however, had a better heart.

"It is wrong," she said, "for us to talk in

202

The Beaver Stick

this way about the young man. He cannot
help being poor, and I am sorry for him. I
must say, though, that he might be cleaner and
neater than he is. I wish I could talk to him;
I would like to tell him some things that would
be for his good."

"Why, you must be in love with him," one
of the girls exclaimed, laughing.

"Well," replied the other, "I pity the poor
young man, and, if my father would allow me,
I would marry him and make a man of him.
All he needs to change his ways is kindness and
teaching."

In the evening New Robe met this girl, Mas-
tah ki—Raven Woman—as she was coming
from the river with a skin of water. Already
he had combed out his hair and washed himself,
and she stared at him in surprise.

"Ah," he said, stopping her in the path.
"To-day I heard your kind words, and have
taken them to my heart. I am going away
to try to earn a name, to try to become a chief.
Pray for me; ask the Sun to help me."

"I will pray for you every day," said the
girl.

"And if I return such a man that no one

need be ashamed of me," he asked, " will you
be my wife?"

" Yes, gladly," she replied. " And now go;
people are looking at us."

The next morning New Robe left the camp.
He did not know where to go, nor what he was
going to do. Something seemed to tell him to
push forward, and that somehow, in some way,
he would be fortunate. He had but little food,
only some tough, dried meat, and his weapons
were poor and of little use; yet he did not fear
that he would starve, or suffer any harm from
the animals or from the enemy.

It was late in the fall, and the nights were
very cold. One evening, after a long day's
tramp, he came to the edge of a broad beaver
pond. Tall, thick grass grew on the dam,
and he pulled armfuls of this and heaped it
up, and then crawled under the pile to pass
the night. It was a warm, soft nest, and he
was already almost asleep when some one called
his name. He lifted his head and looked out
from under the grass, and saw standing near
by a handsome young man, very beautifully
dressed.

" Come," said the stranger, " this is a cold

and cheerless place. My father's lodge is close by, and he asks you to be his guest."

New Robe arose and shook the grass from his robe. "It is strange," he said, "that I did not see your camp. Before I descended into the valley from the prairie I looked carefully over it, up and down."

"It is very near here," the stranger replied. "Come, let us go in. My father waits for us, and the night is cold."

He started, and led the way out over the ice, which had frozen from the shore for some distance out into the pond. New Robe followed, wondering why they should take that course. Presently they reached the edge of the ice; just beyond, a large beaver house rose above the water.

"That is our home," said the stranger. "Now, I am going to dive, and you must follow me. Just shut your eyes, and do not be afraid."

With a great splash he disappeared in the water, and New Robe, after hesitating a little and praying to the Sun for aid in this strange adventure, closed his eyes and pitched headlong into the place where his companion had disappeared. After swimming a few strokes, he felt the pressure of the water suddenly give way, and, opening his eyes, found that he was in a great circular lodge. From the doorway a pool of water extended into the centre of it, and between its edge and the walls were beds of soft and beautiful robes. On the one at the back sat a kind - looking old man, who spoke pleasantly to him and bade him take a seat by his side; and as New Robe stepped out of the pool he found that he was perfectly dry— no part of his clothing or person had been wet by the water he had passed through. Near the old man sat his wife, a handsome old woman, and on other beds reclined their two sons, one of whom had guided New Robe to the place. They all wore clothing of beautiful material and fashion, but he now noticed that the skin of each of these persons, wherever it could be seen—even their faces—was covered with fine fur, that of the two sons being pure white.

"You are welcome, my son," said the old man—"welcome to the lodge of the Beaver Chief. One of my sons saw you creeping into your nest of grass, and I bade him invite you in. These nights are cold for one to be without shelter."

The Beaver Stick

" Yes," added his wife, " and no doubt the poor young man is hungry; he seems to be lean and pinched."

" *Oh! Ai!* To be sure," said the old man; " of course he is hungry: just give me a dish, and I will prepare some food for him."

New Robe looked in astonishment at what the Beaver Chief was doing. He took a large buffalo chip and placed it in the dish, and began to break it up into fine pieces, singing, as he did so, a strange song. The hard, dry stuff turned into rich pemmican, and when the last bit of the chip had been broken up the bowl was passed to him. His wonder increased when he found that the food tasted as good as it looked.

" Our only food," said the old man, " is the bark of the trees; for, after all, you know, we are actually beavers, although we have the power to change our bodies into the form of any living thing. But there are many secret and wonderful things that we have learned through much prayer and through the search for different medicines. Stay with us for a time, and perhaps you may learn something of them. Just look about you and see how many we have gathered in our time."

The Punishment of the Stingy

Indeed, there were more than one could count. They hung on the walls and from the roof, enclosed in beautiful pouches and sacks of strange shape. New Robe wondered what they were, and wished he could open each one and examine it.

The pool in the centre of the lodge was never still; the current coming in from the door whirled slowly around and around. On its surface floated a short piece of beaver cutting which seemed very old and quite water-soaked; yet it did not sink, nor, like other pieces of wood, finally float out on the current constantly entering and going out of the doorway. Night and day it whirled slowly around the circumference of the pool. Although there was no fire in the lodge, it was warm enough, and not colder at night than in the daytime; thus little covering was needed when its occupants went to bed.

New Robe was awakened from his first night's rest in the strange place by the old man calling him to arise and eat. He had scarcely begun to taste a fresh dish of the strangely made pemmican, when the water in the pool began to heave and rise, and then again sank to its level as one of the sons arose from its depths and stepped over to his couch, not a drop of water clinging to him or his garments. "Our pond is frozen over," he said. "Not even an air-hole remains open."

"*Hai!*" the old man exclaimed. "Is it so? Well, winter has come, and," turning to New Robe, "now you cannot leave us until spring comes and melts the ice. But do not be uneasy; we will treat you well, and try to make your life here pleasant."

So New Robe spent the winter in the beaver's lodge. The days came and went, one after another, and easy contentment marked their flight. Most of the waking hours were passed by the beavers in praying to their medicines and in singing their sacred songs, and the young man, listening, learned much of their secret wisdom.

The months passed, and one morning the water in the whirling pool was seen to be a little muddy. The next day, one of the sons reported that in places the ice had melted. The old man and the two sons went out to look about and inspect the dam, leaving New Robe and the old woman inside.

"*Kyi,*" she said, "summer is now come, and

you will soon leave us. Before you go the old man will make you a present; he will give you your choice of all his medicines. Choose that stick whirling about there in the pool, for it is the strongest of them all. He will try to make you believe it is worthless, but insist on having it, and finally he will give it to you."

Presently the others returned. "Well," said the old man to New Robe, "spring has really come, and I know that you wish to return to your people. I am going to give you something to take back with you. Look about you, my son. See all these beautiful medicines hanging on the walls. Choose the one you fancy, and it is yours."

"Give me that," said New Robe, pointing to the floating stick.

"*O-e-ai!*" the old man exclaimed, in a surprised and pained tone. "*O-e-ai!* What? That old stick? Surely, my son, you must be crazy. Look about you; open your eyes and choose one of these beautiful medicines."

"Give me the stick," New Robe repeated.

"Come, come. Surely you do not know what you ask for. Now let me explain to you,"

The Beaver Stick

and the old man began to point out the different medicines and to tell what they were, explaining the wonderful and mysterious power of each. "There, you see," he concluded, "how unreasonable was your choice. Now I have explained them all, tell me which will you have?"

New Robe considered; he wondered if the old woman had not been mistaken in advising him to choose the old beaver cutting, but he caught her eye, and, assured by her meaning glance, replied as before, "Give me the stick."

Once more the old man tried with all his power to persuade him to make a different choice, and the sweat rolled from his brow as he entreated the young man to select something else, and once more New Robe said, "I want the stick."

"*O-e-ai!*" cried the old man in despair. "Four times you have asked for the old cutting, and when that sacred number is reached I cannot refuse. Take the cutting, my son. It is the most valuable and powerful of all my medicines. It is really a beaver which, at will, you can change to the simple cutting as it appears to be."

The Punishment of the Stingy

New Robe was pleased, and when he learned
how powerful the medicine was that he had
chosen he knew that he had not left the home of
his people in vain. He was now obliged to
put off his departure, for he had to learn the
hundred songs and the many prayers that went
with his gift. But at last he knew them all
by heart, and the old man gave him some parting advice.

" You must not look back," he said, " when
you leave us, not even once, or the medicine
will leave you and return to me. Also, you
must always carry it concealed beneath your
shirt, hanging by the string I have tied to it.
Never let any one see it, or your power will be
broken."

Then they all bade him good-bye, and he
dived into the pool, and presently rose to the
surface of the pond. When he reached the
shore he knelt down in the grass and cried,
cried long and bitterly, for he felt very sad to
leave the kind beavers. It was all he could do
to keep from looking back for one last glimpse
of them. But after a time he rose and walked
on, out of the valley, up over the dry, wide
plain. After a little he came to a river,

swollen and swift with the melted snows. He placed a little cutting in the water, and it changed at once into a large, pure white beaver.

"Little brother," said New Robe, "the stream is high and dangerous. Cut me some logs so that I may make a raft on which to cross it safely."

At once the beaver began to fell some trees, and, as fast as he cut them into lengths, New Robe bound them together. In a little while there were enough to bear his weight, and he crossed to the other side in safety. Then, lifting the beaver up, it changed into the stick again, and, putting it safely in his bosom, he journeyed on.

One morning he came in sight of the camp, and sat down on a neighboring hill, prepared to do just as the old man had instructed him.

Pretty soon two or three young men approached, looking with wonder at the strange and beautiful robe he wore. When they had come near enough to hear his voice—for he kept his face covered—he told them to stand where they were, and asked them to go and tell the father of Raven Woman that he was New Robe, returned from strange adventures, and with a powerful medicine. " Ask him," he said, " to have four sweat lodges built for me, in a row from east to west, and when the stones are heated to let me know."

The young men returned to the camp, and in a little while came back to say that all was ready. New Robe told them to walk ahead and warn the people to keep away from him, and, as they all stood in a big crowd on each side of his path, he came to the first sweat lodge and entered it. Sprinkling the water on the hot stones, he began the sacred songs that the old man beaver had taught him, and, as he sang, some of the fur with which his body had been gradually covered during the winter fell to the ground. Soon he left this sweat lodge and went into the next one, and the people crowded around the one he had left, looking with wonder at the little heap of shed fur. So he went into the four sweat lodges, one after the other.

When he came out of the fourth sweat lodge, New Robe had shed the last of his beaver fur, and was so changed that no one recognized him. He was a beautiful, clear-eyed, long-haired young man. He went straight to Raven

The Beaver Stick

Woman, who was standing near, and took her hand. They were both so happy they could not speak. The girl's father pointed to his lodge. " It is yours," he said, " and everything it contains. Go and live happily, my children."

New Robe became a great chief. By the aid of his medicine he was able not only to cure sickness, but he became a great warrior. No river or lake could stop his way, and he was able to kill many of the enemy who were encamped by the shores of any water, for, whenever he asked it of his medicine, it took him safely down under the surface of the water, wherever he wished to go.

Little Friend Coyote

Little Friend Coyote

I T was in the summer, when the Blackfoot and Piegan tribes were camped
together, that the Blackfoot Front
Wolf first noticed Su-yé-sai-pi, a
Piegan girl, and liked her, and determined
to make her his wife. She was young and handsome and of good family, and her parents were
well-to-do, for her father was a leading warrior
of his tribe. Front Wolf was himself a noted
warrior, and had grown rich from his forays
on the camps of the enemy, so when he asked
for the young woman her parents were pleased
—pleased to give their daughter to such a strong
young man, and pleased to accept the thirty
horses he sent them with the request.

In those days, in the long ago, such intertribal marriages were common, for the two great
camps often travelled together in quest of the
buffalo, sometimes for a whole winter and

summer, and thus the young people became acquainted with each other. Again they would be separated by hundreds of miles of rolling plain.

After their marriage the young couple continued to live in the Piegan camp, for Front Wolf had many friends there of his own age, who begged him to remain with them. They liked to go on raids under his leadership better than with any one else. It seemed to his wife as if he were always away on some expedition, so seldom was he at home, and as she had learned to respect and love him, she was very lonely during these long absences. One summer, only two or three days after his return from a successful war-journey against the Crows, he said to his wife: " It is a long time since I have seen my parents. Now I think it time for me to visit them and give them some horses. If you have any little things you wish to send them, hurry and make them ready, so that I may take them."

" I have some pretty moccasins for your father," said Su-yé-sai-pi, " and a fine buckskin dress for your mother; but I am not going to send them. I want to go with you and present them myself. It seems as if you do not care at all for me. Here you are just home from a long journey, and yet you would start right out again, without thinking about me at all."

"No," Front Wolf replied, "it is not that I do not love you; you may go with me if you insist on it. I did not like to ask you to make the trip, for the distance is great, and there is danger on the way."

Su-yé-sai-pi was happy. She began her preparations at once, and only laughed at her parents when they urged her to remain with them, telling her that the plains swarmed with war parties in search of scalps and plunder, and that she would surely be killed.

At this time the Piegans were hunting on the Lower Milk River, but the morning that Front Wolf and his wife started away the whole camp moved too, for the chiefs wished to pass the hot season along the foot-hills of the great mountains. At the last moment five young Blackfeet, visitors in the camp, decided that they too would return home, so they set forth with the couple, and helped drive the little herd of horses that Front Wolf intended to give his relatives. The northern tribe was

thought to be summering on the Red Deer
River, and a course was roughly taken for the
place where it joins the Saskatchewan. This
brought the little party, after three or four
days' travel, to the Cypress Hills, or, as they
were named by the Indians, the Gap-in-the-Mid-
dle Hills. They reached the southern slopes
of the low buttes one morning, after being without water all the preceding day, and prepared
to camp and rest at the edge of a little grove,
close to which a large, clear spring bubbled
up from a pile of sunken bowlders. They did
not know that a large camp of Kutenais was just
behind the hills where they stopped, and that
one of their hunters, seeing them coming, had
hurried home and spread the news. Su-yé-sai-
pi had scarcely started a fire when the warriors
from the camp were seen to be approaching
the little party from all directions, completely
hemming them in. Although these two tribes,
the Blackfeet and Kutenais, had once been very
friendly to each other, they were now at war.
When the strangers approached, one of them,
the chief, who had learned Blackfoot in other
days, called out, " Don't fire; we are friends;
we will not harm you."

Little Friend Coyote

Front Wolf and his friends had drawn the covers from their guns, prepared to fight and to sell their lives dearly, but when Front Wolf heard this, and saw that the strangers made no motions to shoot, he lowered his rifle and said: "They intend to make peace with us; I guess they are tired of being at war with our people. Do not be afraid; they will not harm us."

The chief came up first, and shook hands with Front Wolf and the rest, saying: "I am glad to meet you. Our camp is near. Come over to my lodge, and we will feast and smoke."

These were kind words. The little party of Blackfeet did not doubt that they were sincere. They packed up again, mounted their horses, and rode around the hill to the lodges. The chief invited them to stop with him, and they rode towards the big lodge in the centre of the village, where many people were gathered. There they dismounted, when suddenly their arms were taken from them by the surrounding crowd, and they were pushed into the big lodge. It was a very hot day, and all around the skin lodge-covering had been raised to allow the cool breeze to pass beneath it, so the prisoners could see all that was happening without. Their little band of horses was quickly divided and led away; and then the chief and all the men had a long talk.

Presently the chief came inside and sat down in his accustomed place at the back of the lodge. Following him four warriors entered, and seizing the young Blackfoot who sat nearest the door, led him out some little distance from the lodge, where one of them brained him with a war-club, and then every one tried to get a piece of his scalp or to plunge a knife into his body. In a moment his hands, feet, and head were severed, and women were pushing and kicking and pounding the mutilated parts here and there, singing as they did so the shrill song of revenge. The Blackfeet looked on at this terrible butchery of their friend with horror, but in stolid silence, all save Su-yé-sai-pi, who gave a frightened cry when she saw the poor fellow struck down, and, clasping her husband by the arm, buried her face in his breast. The chief smiled, but did not speak. Presently another one of the young Blackfeet was led out, and met the fate of the first one. One after another, when his turn came, each arose and accompanied his captors without struggle or cry, and met his death as a warrior should.

At last all had been killed except Front Wolf and his wife, and presently they came for him. Su-yé-sai-pi clung to him and cried and begged, but her husband himself put her from him and went out, saying to her a last kind word. "Do not cry," he said. "Take courage. Take courage." As he neared the place of butchery he began to sing his war-song, and the poor wife, looking on, saw him smile as the great stone club descended, and he fell forward lifeless to the ground. The woman now thought that her turn had come, but the executioners did not return. She wished that they would not delay; she wished to have the dreadful ordeal over with, so that her shadow might overtake her husband's as it travelled along on the road to the Sandhills—home of the departed Blackfeet. All the Kutenais, even the women and children, had now painted their faces black, and were dancing the scalp-dance, carrying before them the scalps, stretched on long, forked willows.

"Come," said the chief to Su-yé-sai-pi, of-

The Punishment of the Stingy

fering her the scalp from Front Wolf's head—
" come, join us in this dance and be happy."

" You may kill me," the woman replied,
" but you cannot make me dance. I beg you to
kill me, so I may join my husband."

The Kutenai laughed. " You are too young
to die yet," he said; " and, besides, we do not
kill women. Before long we are going to make
peace with the Blackfeet and Piegans, and when
that time comes we will give you back to your
people."

Of course it was a lie, for he had no thought
of making peace, but intended to keep the
woman.

Su-yé-sai-pi was very sad. If she sat in the
lodge, the scalp-song rang in her ears; if she
stepped outside, the bodies of her husband and
friends greeted her eyes. She could do nothing
but cry and wish for death to take her.

Several days passed, and the rejoicings of the
camp still continued. One afternoon an old
widow woman called her into a poor little lodge
and said: " I have great pity for you, and will
do what I can to help you. I do not know what
the chief has decided to do with you, but, whatever it is, I would save you from it. Your

"SU-YE SAI-PI CLUNG TO HIM"

only chance is to try to get away from here in the night and seek your people. I will fill a good big pouch with dried meat and pemmican, and some moccasins, and as soon as it is dark I will place it behind my lodge. When the people are all asleep, and the evening fire has died out, leave your bed as quietly as you can, pick up the pouch, and hurry away in the direction from which you came."

Su-yé-sai-pi burst out crying. No one had been kind to her before, and kindness made her cry. She kissed her new friend, and when she could speak she said that she would try to get away that night. It seemed as if night would never come, and then as if the people would never stop talking and feasting and go to bed. But at last everything was quiet in the camp, and in the chief's lodge the fire of small willows had died down, and the deep breathing of the occupants showed that they were asleep. The captive cautiously arose from her couch near the door and stole outside. She stood and listened a moment, and then coughed once or twice. No one moved inside; so, feeling sure that no one was watching her, or had noticed her come out, she went to the widow's lodge, and found the pouch behind it, and quickly but noiselessly left the camp.

The sky was overcast, and presently heavy rain, with thunder and lightning, came up, but she walked swiftly, steadily on, not knowing nor caring whither, so long as it was away from her enemies. The shower passed, and the moon came out, and then the poor woman heard shouts and calls, and the rushing tread of horses; the whole camp was aroused, and they were searching for her. She crouched in the shadow of a bowlder, and heard horsemen go by on either side. Once two or three of them rode by in plain sight. She remained there a long time, until everything was still again, and then hurried on. In a little while she approached a small lake, and saw three horses by its edge.

"Here," she said to herself, "would be a good chance if I only had a rope. Perhaps they are hobbled; if so, the thongs will do for a bridle." She walked carefully nearer, when suddenly she saw three dim figures on the ground and heard a loud snore. She almost fainted with fright, knowing that these were some of her pursuers waiting for daylight to resume their search. Quick as a flash she stooped among the low brush, crawled slowly back, and then, rising, hurried away in another direction.

In a little while day began to break, and she found herself on a wide plain south of the hills. In a little ravine near by there was an old wolf den; she crawled down into it, feet foremost, first carefully obliterating her footsteps in the soft, loose earth about it. There she remained all day, eating none of her little store of food, for she was so thirsty it choked her. Several times during the day she heard the distant tramp of horses, but she did not look out, much as she wished to see what was going on.

When darkness came once more, she climbed out and started in search of water, not knowing which way to look for it, or whether she would ever find any. She travelled on, and on, and on, and, when daylight again brightened the sky, found herself at the place where her husband lay. Yes, there were the bodies of him and his friends, now shapeless and terrible objects. And the Kutenais were gone. Fearing that she might find her people, dreading the awful vengeance that would overtake them if

229

The Punishment of the Stingy

she did, they were no doubt already fleeing towards the pine-covered slopes of the great mountains. Worn out from her long tramp, and nearly crazed from thirst, the poor woman had barely strength to go on to the spring, where she drank long of the cool water, and then fell asleep.

The sun was hot, but Su-yé-sai-pi slept on. Well on in the afternoon she was awakened by something nudging her side. "They have found me," she said to herself, shivering with terror, "and when I move a knife will be thrust in my side." She lay motionless a little while, and then could bear the suspense no longer; slowly rising up and turning back her robe, what should she find lying by her side but a coyote, looking up into her face and wagging his tail!

"Oh, little wolf!" she cried. "Oh, little brother! Have pity on me. You know the wide plains; lead me to my people, for my husband is killed, and I am lost."

The little animal kept wagging his tail, and when she arose and went again to the spring, he followed her. She drank, and then ate a little dried meat, not forgetting to give him

"'OH, LITTLE WOLF!' SHE CRIED"

some, which he hastily devoured. She talked to him all the time, telling him what had happened, and what she wished to do; and he seemed to understand, for when she started to leave the spring he bounded on ahead, often stopping and looking back, as much as to say, " Come on; this is the way."

They were passing through the broken hills, and the coyote, quite a long way ahead, had climbed to the top of a low butte and looked cautiously over it, when he turned, ran back part way, and then circled off to the right. Su-yé-sai-pi was frightened, thinking he had sighted the Kutenais, and she ran after him as fast as she could go. He led her to the top of another hill, and then, looking away along the ridge, she saw that he had led her around a band of grizzly bears, feeding and playing on the steep slope. Then she knew for certain that he was to be trusted, and she told him to keep a long way ahead, to look over the country from every rise of ground, and to warn her if he saw anything suspicious. This he did. He would wait for her at the top of a ridge, where they would sit and rest awhile, and as soon as she was ready to go on he would run to the top of the next rise before she had taken fifty steps. If thirsty, she would tell him, and in a little while he would always take her to some water. Sometimes it would be a small trickling stream in a coulée; sometimes a soft, damp gravel-bed, where she was obliged to scoop out a hole; sometimes it was a muddy buffalo-wallow—and it was always strong with alkali —but it was the best there was.

In this way, after many days, they came to the Little (Milk) River. The pouch had long been empty, and Su-yé-sai-pi was weak from hunger, and her weary feet were swollen and blistered, for the last pair of moccasins had been worn out. Here by the river were plenty of berries and some roots that are often eaten —good to fill the belly, but not strength-making food. Of them she ate all she could, and frequently bathed her feet, and kept on up the valley; but every day she went more slowly. The stops for rest were more frequent now, and the coyote showed that he was beginning to feel uneasy. When he thought she had sat still too long, he would whine and paw at her dress, and look away up the stream, urging her to go on. He himself fared well on the ground-squirrels and prairie-dogs he managed to catch, and often he brought one to her; but she could not bring herself to eat it raw, and she had no way of building a fire to roast it.

One day, while the sun was hottest, the two stopped to rest in a thick patch of brush. They were near the mountains now, and the valley was wide, with low, sloping hills on either side. The woman had been telling her companion—she talked to him now as she would have talked to a person—that her feet were swollen so badly she could go no farther, and then she fell asleep. She was awakened by the coyote jerking her gown and whining, and she sat up and listened. Pretty soon she heard people talking; they were some distance away, but the murmur of their voices seemed familiar; they came nearer, and she heard one say, in her own language, " Let's cross the river here."

She hobbled out to the edge of the brush and called to them, and when they rode up to where she stood, at first they did not know her, she was so worn and thin. She told them her story, and pointed to the coyote by her side, telling them how it had helped her, and begging them not to kill it. They told her that the camp was only a little way above on the river, and offered her a horse to ride, but she asked them to go on and tell her mother to come after her with a travois, for she felt too sore to ride. Presently her mother came, and her father, and a great throng of the people, and when she saw them approaching she put her arms around the coyote and kissed him.

"You have saved my life," she said; "and much as I grieve to, we must part now, for, while I might prevent the people from harming you, I could not stop the camp dogs from tearing you to pieces. But do not go far away. Every time we move camp my father's lodge shall be the last to go; and when the rest and the dogs have all left, we will leave food for you where our lodge stood. We will always do that."

The coyote seemed to understand. He licked her face and whined, and as her mother and father approached he slowly moved away, looking back many, many times.

Su-yé-sai-pi cried—cried at parting with her faithful guide, and because at sight of her mother all her trials and sufferings came back to her mind. They placed her on the travois and drew her to camp, where all the people came to sympathize with her, bringing something from their store of choice food as presents.

The coyote was not forgotten; food was always left at the camp site, as she had promised, and often, as Su-yé-sai-pi and her people started on after the others, they saw him standing on a near hill, watching them out of sight.

THE END